Nottingham Playhouse Theatre Company
presents the UK premiere of

THE LEAGUE OF YOUTH

BY HENRIK IBSEN
IN A NEW VERSION BY ANDY BARRETT

D0168233

Supported by

NORWEGIAN EMBASSY

First performed at Nottingham Playhouse on
Friday 13 May 2011

Nottingham Playhouse Theatre Company
presents the UK premiere of

THE LEAGUE OF YOUTH

BY HENRIK IBSEN, IN A NEW VERSION BY ANDY BARRETT

LUNDESTAD	**David Acton**
DR FJELDBO	**Russell Bentley**
CHAMBERLAIN BRATSBERG	**Philip Bretherton**
STENSGARD	**Sam Callis**
THORA BRATSBERG	**Bridie Higson**
ASLAKSEN	**Mark Jardine**
MONSEN	**Robin Kingsland**
ERIK BRATSBERG/ BASTIAN MONSEN	**Chris Nayak**
DANIEL HEIRE	**Jon Rumney**
MADAM RUNDHOLM	**Debra Stewart**
SELMA BRATSBERG/ RAGNA MONSEN	**Victoria Yeates**

Townspeople and Servants – **Nic Adams, Sarah Astill, Alexandra Bradley, Liam Butlin, Angus Drakeford, Robert Goll, Hannah Hall, Mark Jarvis, Sean Kelly, Leo Lanzoni, James McMahon, Nick Newman, Sally Nix, Lindsey Parr, Natasha Stewart**

Director	**Giles Croft**
Designer	**Dawn Allsopp**
Lighting Designer	**Alexandra Stafford**
Composer/Sound Designer	**Matthew Bugg**
Adapter	**Andy Barrett**
Literal Translator	**Charlotte Barslund**
Assistant Director	**Martin Berry**
Company and Stage Manager	**Jane Eliot-Webb**
Deputy Stage Manager	**Stuart Lambert**
Assistant Stage Manager	**Kathryn Bainbridge-Wilson**
Stage Management Work Placement	**Jenna Price**

Cast

David Acton (Lundestad)

David trained at Webber Douglas Academy of Dramatic Arts.

Previously for Nottingham Playhouse: *I Have Been Here Before*, *The Burial at Thebes*, *Vertigo*.

Other theatre credits include: seasons at Bolton, Durham, York, Basingstoke, Southampton, Chester, Watford and Cherub Company; *Hamlet* (Oxford Playhouse); *The Clandestine Marriage* (Bristol Old Vic); *Romeo and Juliet*, *A Midsummer Night's Dream* (AFTLS USA tours); *Othello*, *Henry V*, *The Comedy of Errors*, *Twelfth Night*, *A Midsummer Night's Dream* (Propeller, Watermill, Newbury and international tours); *Down By the Greenwood Side* (Donmar Warehouse); *King Lear* (Young Vic, London, Leicester Haymarket and Tokyo Globe); *Caesar and Cleopatra* (Greenwich); *Celaine* (Hampstead, London); *Celestina* (Birmingham Rep and Edinburgh International Festival); *Much Ado About Nothing* (Peter Hall Company); *Copenhagen*, *Relatively Speaking* (Watermill, Newbury); *Richard II* (Old Vic, London); *One Night in November* (Belgrade, Coventry); *Sabbat*, *Jason and the Argonauts*, *Peter Pan* (Dukes, Lancaster); *Anjin* (Tokyo); *House of Ghosts* (national tour); *How to Be Happy* (one-man show).

Credits for the RSC include: *The Constant Couple*, *The Man of Mode*, *King Lear*, *Hamlet*, *The Comedy of Errors*, *The Love of the Nightingale*, *As You Like It*, *Henry V*, *Edward III*, *Eastward Ho!*, *The Roman Actor* (RSC Jacobethan Season also at Gielgud Theatre).

Television credits include: *EastEnders*, *I Love Keith Allen*, *All in the Game*, *So Haunt Me*, *Persuasion*, *Casualty*, *Randall and Hopkirk (Deceased)*, *The Wyvern Mystery*, *Macbeth*, *Fooling Hitler*, *Casanova's Love Letters*, *Class of '76*, *Blair on Trial*, *Doctors*, *Tchaikovsky*, *The Bill*, *Hollyoaks*, *Passage*, *Silent Witness*.

Russell Bentley (Dr Fjeldbo)

Russell trained at Central School of Speech and Drama.

Theatre credits include: *Drowning on Dry Land* (Jermyn Street, London); *Life After* (New End, London); *Death of a Salesman* (West Yorkshire Playhouse); *Six Characters in Search of an Author* (Headlong, Bristol Old Vic and No 1 UK tour); *3 Sisters on Hope Street* (Liverpool Everyman and Hampstead, London); *Sit and Shiva* (Hackney Empire); *Chicken Soup with Barley* (Nottingham Playhouse and Tricycle, London); *Violent B* (Royal Court young writers' scheme); *Old Wicked Songs* (Bristol Old Vic and Gielgud, London); *Tower of Bagel* (Soho, London); *Roaring Lions* (Lyric Hammersmith); *Angel* (Old Vic: Old Vic New Voices Season); *Spoils of War* (Young Vic); *Bitter Fruits of Palestine* (John Caird Company) *Waiting for Lefty*, *The Cradle Will Rock* (Battersea Arts Centre); *Destiny of Me*, *Patience* (Finborough, London).

Television credits include: *Footballers' Wives*, *EastEnders*, *The Bill*, *The Eustace Brothers*, *Joy to the World*, *Clitheroe*, *Cuban Conflict in America*.

Film credits include: *Kick-Ass*, *Proof*, *Below*, *Biodiversity*, *Lone Clouds*, *Lost Battalion*, *Carmela*.

Radio credits include: *Normandy*, *The Other Man*, *Women's Hour*, *Voyage* (Sony Award for Best Drama), *The Whore of Mensa*, *Disordered Minds*, *Goal*, *Ring Around the Bath* (all BBC).

Audiobooks include: *The Time Traveler's Wife*, *Homage*.

Philip Bretherton (Chamberlain Bratsberg)

Philip last appeared at Nottingham Playhouse in *Breaking the Silence*.

Other theatre credits include: *Hay Fever* (West Yorkshire Playhouse); *Blackthorn, Pygmalion, An Ideal Husband, Present Laughter, Blithe Spirit, Noises Off, The Importance of Being Earnest* (Theatr Clwyd); *Who's Afraid of Virginia Woolf? Six Degrees of Separation* (Manchester Royal Exchange); *Life After Scandal* (Hampstead, London); *Joan of Arc* (Birmingham Rep); *Beethoven's Tenth, Darkness Falls* (Watford Palace); *Private Lives* (Citizens, Glasgow); *Skylight* (Stephen Joseph, Scarborough).

Television credits include: Ian Davenport in *Coronation Street*; Football Manager, Stefan Hauser in *Footballers' Wives*; Dr Bower in *Casualty,* Alistair Deacon in nine series of *As Time Goes By.*

Other television credits include: *Silk, Midsomer Murders, The Bill, Murder in Suburbia, New Tricks, Doctors, Swallow, Hearts and Bones, Real Women, Family Affairs, Wing and a Prayer, Hollyoaks, Sharman, Sherlock Holmes, The Veiled One, The Paradise Club, Inspector Morse, Miss Marple: At Bertram's Hotel.*

He also appeared in the film *Cry Freedom* and most recently in *Dark Floors*.

Radio credits include: several plays for BBC Radio 4.

Sam Callis (Stensgard)

Sam trained at LAMDA.

Theatre credits include: Titania in *A Midsummer Night's Dream* (Brooklyn Academy of Music, New York); Sergius in *Arms and the Man* (No 1 UK tour); Ferdinand in *The Tempest* (Sheffield Crucible and Old Vic, London); Florizel in *The Winter's Tale* (Salisbury Playhouse); *Twelfth Night* (Watermill, Newbury); *Druff* (Tristan Bates, London); Antipholus in *The Comedy of Errors* (Pleasance and international tour); *Henry V* (Watermill, Newbury and international tour); *Misalliance* (Theatr Clwyd and Birmingham Rep); *Squealing Like a Pig* (Birmingham Rep).

Television credits include: *Holby City, The Bill, The Royal, Ultimate Force IV, Dr Who, London's Burning.*

Film credits include: *Kidulthood, Trance, Capital Punishment, Shrink.*

Bridie Higson (Thora Bratsberg)

Bridie recently graduated from Manchester's Arden School of Theatre with a first class honours degree in Acting. She is thrilled to be making her professional stage debut in her hometown at Nottingham Playhouse in *The League of Youth*. Her credits during her training include Viola in *Twelfth Night*, Stage Manager in *Our Town* and Selby in *The After-Dinner Joke.*

Mark Jardine (Aslaksen)

After training at the East 15 School of Acting, Mark made his professional debut in the national tour of *Grease* playing the role of Kenickie. He followed this with *Oklahoma!* at the Liverpool Everyman and Playhouse, the lead in *City of Angels* in Yeovil and then a national tour of the musical *Patsy Cline*, which transferred to London's West End.

The following year Mark was on tour again playing Mr Lyons in the hugely successful revival of *Blood Brothers*, a role he later reprised in the West End. He then travelled to Hamburg to play Tom in *Table Manners* and returned to London for the world premiere of *The Famous Five: the Musical* in which he played Mr Thomas. He followed this with the titular role in *The Wizard of Oz* at the Wales Millennium Centre, the role of Daddy in the world premiere of *The Problem With Being It* at the Castle Theatre, Wellingborough and Captain Hook in *Peter Pan* at the Chelmsford Civic Theatre. Mark is also a member of Lichfield Garrick Theatre Repertory Company where he has played Judd in *Bouncers*, Vladimir in *Waiting for Godot* and Landlord in Jim Cartwright's *Two.*

Television credits include: series regular Phil Weston in *Emmerdale* and roles in *Donovan*, *Hollyoaks*, *The Royal*, *Coronation Street*, *Diamond Geezers*, *Dr Who*, *Barbara* and *The New Adventures of Robin Hood*.

Film credits include: the Ian Curtis biopic *Control* and Jim Loach's *Oranges and Sunshine*, both of which were shot partly in Nottingham.

Mark's association with the Nottingham Playhouse began in 2009 with the role of Danny in *Garage Band* written by Nottingham playwright Andy Barrett. In 2010 he toured in another Barrett play, *The Story Traders of Sichuan*, with the Flying Panda Company and returned to the Playhouse as Mr Jardine in *Forever Young* – a role he has just reprised in the current season.

Robin Kingsland (Monsen)

Theatre credits include: leading roles in the premiere of *Cardenio – The Lost Shakespeare*, *Dick Barton – Quantum of Porridge* (Croydon Warehouse); *On the Waterfront* (Nottingham Playhouse, Edinburgh Fringe, West End and Hong Kong Arts Festival); *Rat Pack Confidential* (Nottingham Playhouse and West End); *Garage Band*, *The Price*, *I Have Been Here Before*, *The Secret Garden* (Nottingham Playhouse); the four interconnected Worcester Century Plays (Swan, Worcester); *Lady Windermere's Fan* (Wolsey, Ipswich); *Loot*, *She Stoops to Conquer*, *Rookery Nook*, *The Return of the Native*, *Man of the Moment*, *I Have Been Here Before* (Mercury, Colchester).

West End credits include: *High Society*, *Lennon*, *Blood Brothers*, *The Cabinet Minister* and playing troubled Rat-packer Peter Lawford in the West End transfer of Nottingham Playhouse's production of *Rat Pack Confidential*.

For radio Robin played Fr. Bardolino in *Deceit of Angels* (Radio 4). He has also appeared on numerous audiobooks including playing Dr Adam Hope in the *Animal Ark* series.

He played Prof. Henry Barker in the CBBC Drama *The Sparticle Mystery* and has also appeared in *The Bill* and *Casualty*.

Robin is delighted to be back at a theatre with which he has a long and happy association, and working on such an exciting project.

Chris Nayak (Erik Bratsberg/Bastian Monsen)

Chris trained at Bristol Old Vic Theatre School.

Previously at Nottingham Playhouse: Tony Lumpkin in *She Stoops to Conquer* and George in *Arthur & George* in 2010.

Other theatre credits include: *East is East* (Birmingham Rep); *Invasion!* (Soho, London); *Romeo and Juliet*, *Lisa's Sex Strike* (Northern Broadsides); *Indian Ink* (Salisbury Playhouse); *A Passage to India* (Shared Experience UK and US tour); *The Marriage of Figaro* (Tara Arts); *Beastly Tales* (Licketyspit Theatre); *East Is East* (York Theatre Royal, Pilot Theatre); *Mother Goose and the Wolf* (Greenwich); *Punchkin: Enchanter* (London Bubble); *Twelfth Night*, *The Taming of the Shrew* (Crwys Theatre).

Television credits include: *Coronation Street*, *Primeval*, *Love Soup*, *Doctors*, *Judge John Deed*, *The Bill*, *Casualty*.

Jon Rumney (Daniel Heire)

Jon started his career in weekly rep at the Old Castle Theatre in Farnham. He has worked at the National Theatre playing Dr Gottlieb in *Ghetto* and King Ferdinand in *Fuente Ovejuna*, the latter touring to the Edinburgh Festival, Spain and Ireland. Previous work at Nottingham Playhouse has been as the furniture dealer Solomon in Arthur Miller's *The Price* and Copin in *Ritual in Blood*.

Musical theatre credits include: the Rabbi in *Fiddler on the Roof* alongside Chaim Topol (London Palladium and tour); *Maddie* (Salisbury and Lyric, West End); *Sophie Tucker* (New End, London); Lazar Wolf in *Fiddler on the Roof* (West Yorkshire Playhouse).

Other theatre credits include: Peter Hall's production of *Orpheus Descending* (Theatre Royal Haymarket); Capulet in *Romeo and Juliet* (Young Vic, UK tour and Amsterdam); *The Miser, Murder Dear Watson* (Churchill, Bromley); *Richard II, A Passage to India* (Bristol Old Vic); *An Enemy of the People* (Oxford Playhouse); *The Barber of Seville, Black Comedy, The Picture of Dorian Gray* (Watford Palace); Shylock in *The Merchant of Venice* (Phoenix, Chelmsford).

During four seasons at the Edinburgh Festival, parts ranged from Pirandello's The Man with the Flower in his Mouth to Groucho Marx. As Groucho Marx, Jon toured the UK and Canada and a television version of the show was produced for Channel 4 Comedy Hour.

Television credits include: *Goering's Last Stand, Doctors, The Way We Live Now*, three roles in *The Bill, Ashenden, Love Hurts, Wish Me Luck, Juliet Bravo, Sorrell & Son, Coriolanus, Maigret, Beau Geste, The Professionals, Invasion, Wings, Dylan Thomas, The Day of the Triffids, Hogarth, Tycoon, Madson*.

Film credits include: *Sky Captain and the World of Tomorrow, Wondrous Oblivion, Hilary and Jackie, Eleni, Hannah's War, Esther Kahn, Space*.

Debra Stewart (Madam Rundholm)

After graduating from Birmingham School of Acting, Debra landed the lead role in the national tour of *You Strike the Woman* with the Hexagon Theatre in Birmingham. Subsequent roles have included Elmire in Jenny Stephens' production of *Tartuffe* at the Old Rep Theatre in Birmingham and the part of Sarah Maliston in the UK premiere of *Resting (An Actor Despairs!)* at the Everyman Theatre in Cheltenham. She was cast as Dede in Paulette Randall's adaptation of *Dido* at Birmingham Repertory Theatre and has had several roles in various BBC radio dramas.

Victoria Yeates (Selma Bratsberg/Ragna Monsen)

Victoria trained at RADA.

Theatre credits include: Poppy in *Noises Off* (New Wolsey, Ipswich); Poppy in *Rookery Nook* (Menier Chocolate Factory); Frances in *Wuthering Heights* (Birmingham Rep and UK tour); *Killing Alan* (rehearsed reading at Theatre503); various scripts for NFTS (Soho, London); *Wedlock* (rehearsed reading for Tristram Shapeero); *Walking on Water* (White Bear, London); *Don Juan Comes Back from the War, Pains of Youth* (Belgrade, Coventry); workshop of *Perfect Sandcastles* (Hampstead, London); *Dying City* (Battersea Arts Centre); *Days of Hope* (King's Head, London); workshop of *Posh* (Royal Court, London); *Listening Out* (Theatre503); *Big Love* (Gate, London); *The Beard* (Old Red Lion, London).

Television credits include: Sheena in *Holby City* (BBC); Janet in *Lip Service* (Kudos Film on BBC3).

Film credits include: Aida in *Sweetness Follows* (Steel Mill Pictures Ltd).

Radio credits include: *Dante's Inferno* for BBC Radio 4 (Art and Adventure).

For more information please visit www.colekitchenn.com.

Creatives

Andy Barrett *(Adapter)*

This is Andy's third main-stage show for Nottingham Playhouse following on from *The Day that Kevin Came* and *Garage Band*. He has also written a number of shows for the touring theatre company New Perspectives, including *The Allotment*, which was shortlisted for the Amnesty International Freedom of Expression Award, and *Dolly*, the cloning meets country and western musical. Other stage work includes *The Story Traders of Sichuan*, a dual-language play which was created in collaboration with the Sichuan Opera Troupe of Chengdu; *Tales from the Robin Hood Line*, a series of dramatic monologues looking at the implications of pit closures on community life, which he performed in Miners Welfares across Nottinghamshire and Derbyshire; and *The King of Spin* for Leicester Haymarket, which was performed at Bosworth Field.

As Artistic Director (with Julian Hanby) of Hanby and Barrett he has written over twenty community plays which have been performed in towns and villages across the region, often in striking and unusual locations, involving hundreds of local people. *Napkin Café* took over the concourse and PA system of Nottingham Railway Station; *The Vital Spark* was performed on and around a Napoleonic blast furnace; and *The Cries of Silent Men*, which was originally performed at Beauvale Priory, is to be restaged as part of neat11 festival. For more information on this work go to www.hanbyandbarrett.com.

His work for radio includes the Sony Award-winning *Lily's Years*, the afternoon plays *Upton Women*, *The Perfect Wood*, and *The Romantics*, the Women's Hour serial *World of Margaret* and an adaptation of *The Adventures and Farther Adventures of Robinson Crusoe* for the Classic Serial slot.

Giles Croft *(Director)*

Giles started his career as a playwright. In 1985 he was appointed Artistic Director of the Gate Theatre, London. In 1989 Giles joined the National Theatre as Literary Manager. He became Artistic Director of the Palace Theatre, Watford in May 1995.

Giles has been Artistic Director of Nottingham Playhouse since 1999. His productions during that time include *Wonderful Tennessee*, *Because it's There*, *The Boy Who Fell into a Book*, *Polygraph*, *Ethel and Ernest*, *Rat Pack Confidential* (which won the City Life Award for Best Production, toured the UK and transferred to the West End), *The Day that Kevin Came*, *The Man Who*, *Double Indemnity*, *Angels Among the Trees*, *Chicken Soup with Barley* (which transferred to London's Tricycle Theatre), *The White Album*, *To Reach the Clouds*, *Whisky Galore!* (also a UK tour), *I Have Been Here Before*, *Beast on the Moon*, *Vertigo*, *All Quiet on the Western Front*, *The Price*, a co-production with Liverpool Everyman and Playhouse, *Blithe Spirit*, *Garage Band*, *Forever Young*, *The Families of Lockerbie*.

Giles has had plays premiered at The New End, Upstream, and the Finborough Theatres in London as well as in Colchester, Watford, Nottingham and Hull. His adaptations of *Kind Hearts and Coronets*, *The Ladykillers*, *Passport To Pimlico* and *Whisky Galore* have toured widely and been produced throughout the UK and Europe. Most recently his adaptation of *Loving April* from the novel by Melvyn Burgess was toured by Oxfordshire Theatre Company.

Giles also serves as vice-chair of the European Theatre Convention, of which Nottingham Playhouse is a member.

Dawn Allsopp (*Designer*)

Nottingham Playhouse credits include: *Blithe Spirit*, *The Price* (a co-production with Liverpool Everyman and Playhouse), *Beast on the Moon*, *Chicken Soup with Barley*.

Recent theatre credits include: costume designs for *Jack and the Beanstalk* (York Theatre Royal); *The Grapes of Wrath* (Mercury, Colchester); *The Importance of Being Earnest* (New Wolsey, Ipswich); *Town* (Theatre Royal, Northampton); *The Hired Man and Oliver Twist* (Octagon, Bolton); *A Pair of Pinters* (Derby Live); *Beautiful House* (Library Theatre, Manchester); *Fireflies* (The Lowry).

Other theatre credits include: *A Chorus of Disapproval* (New Wolsey, Ipswich and Mercury, Colchester); *Accidental Death of an Anarchist* (Northern Broadsides); *A Glass Menagerie*, *A Funny Thing Happened On the Way to the Forum*, *Sugar* (a co-production with Theatr Clwyd), *Company*, *Neville's Island*; and the sets for *Sleeping Beauty*, *Dick Whittington* (New Wolsey, Ipswich); *Twelfth Night*, *The Homecoming*, *Death of a Salesman*, *A Taste of Honey*, *Private Lives*, *Abandonment*, *A Passionate Woman*, *A Midsummer Night's Dream*, *Les Liaisons Dangereuses*, *The Blue Room*, *The Three Musketeers*, *Closer* (York Theatre Royal); *If I Were You*, *Private Lives*, *Rosencrantz and Guildenstern are Dead*, *Speed the Plow*, *The Price*, *Beyond Belief – Scenes from the Shipman Enquiry* (Library, Manchester); *Quartet*, *How the Other Half Loves*, *Feed*, *Perfect Days*, *Be My Baby*, *Brighton Beach Memoirs*, *The Steamie*, *Sleeping Beauty* (Coliseum, Oldham); *Road*, *Spring and Port Wine*, *A Christmas Carol*, *Shining City*, *Kindertransport*, *Second from Last in the Sack Race*, *Of Mice and Men*, *All of You Mine*, *Misconceptions* (Octagon, Bolton); *The Caretaker* (Dukes, Lancaster); *Only a Matter of Time* (Watermill, Newbury); *Road* (Pilot Theatre/ Lyric Hammersmith).

Dawn is currently an Associate Artist for York Theatre Royal's In the Round season.

Charlotte Barslund (*Literal Translator*)

Charlotte is a Scandinavian translator. She has translated books by Peter Adolphsen, Mikkel Birkegaard, Izzet Celasin, Thomas Enger, Karin Fossum, Sissel-Jo Gazan and Carsten Jensen as well as a wide range of classic and contemporary plays. Her translation of Strindberg's *The Pelican* was broadcast on BBC Radio 3. She is the author of the chapter on literary prose translation in the forthcoming *Oxford Handbook of Translation Studies*. Her translation of *I Curse the River of Time* by Per Petterson is short listed for the 2011 Independent Foreign Fiction Prize.

Martin Berry (*Assistant Director*)

Martin trained at Rose Bruford College in London.

Credits as a director include: *Joseph and the Amazing Technicolor Dreamcoat* (West End); *Rough Guide*, *Send In the Clown* (Jermyn Street, London); *Terrorism* (Greenwich Playhouse); *Oh! What a Lovely War*, *Kiss Me Kate* (Grantham Guildhall); *The Mod Crop* and *Make Do and Mend* (Nottingham Theatre Royal); *Sweeney Todd*, *A Christmas Carol*, *HR'd Day's Night*, *Star Destroyer*, *Kiss of the Spiderwoman*, *Loot*, and a new adaptation of *A Christmas Carol* (awarded in the *Evening Post* top ten productions of the year).

Future projects include: *Into the Woods* at Lakeside Arts Centre, *HR'd Day's Night* at the Edinburgh Festival Fringe 2011, and The *Complete Works of Shakespeare* (*abridged*).

Acting credits include: *Joseph and the Amazing Technicolor Dreamcoat* (West End and tour); Eddie in *Blood Brothers* (tour); Narrator in *Only Love* (Theatre By The Lake); lead vocalist in *Send in the Clown* (off-West End); Jesus in *Godspell* (Playhouse, London); Joe in *A Rough Guide to the Musicals* (off-West End and tour); Professor in *The Lesson* (USA); Andy in *Gregory's Girl* (USA); Les in Berkoff's *East* and Etherege in *The Libertine* (West End); Killer in *The Handmaid's Tale* (English National Opera at the London Coliseum); Inspector in *Revenge* (No 1 tour); Policeman in *Forbidden Love* (No 1 tour); William in *Wicked Bitches* (No 1 tour and Apollo Hammersmith) and Lord Chamberlain in *Cinderella* (Broadway Theatre).

Martin is also a lecturer in Shakespeare, voice and performance at Leicester De Montfort University and in voice and public speaking at Nottingham University.

Matthew Bugg (*Composer/Sound Designer*)

Matthew has just written and directed his first musical *Miss Nightingale*, which was a sell-out success at the Lowry Theatre, before breaking box-office records during its London transfer at the King's Head. He is reviving the production as a regional tour and in the West End in 2012. For more information visit www.missnightingale.co.uk.

Matthew is probably best remembered by Nottingham Playhouse audiences for playing Ariel in *The Tempest*, but his work as composer and sound designer for the Playhouse includes *All Quiet on the Western Front*, *To Reach the Clouds*, *Because it's There*, *The Day that Kevin Came*, *The Hound of the Baskervilles*, *The Mill on the Floss*, *Double Indemnity*, *Wonderful Tennessee*, *Polygraph*.

Other theatre credits include: *Verdict*, *Lark Rise to Candleford* (Bill Kenwright UK tour); *Quartet*, *The Hound of the Baskervilles*, *The Secret of Sherlock Holmes* (Ian Fricker Productions, UK tour and West End); *Northanger Abbey*, *Jamaica Inn* (Salisbury Playhouse and UK tour); *The Invention of Love*, *Barbarians*, *Secret Rapture* (Salisbury Playhouse); *Vanity Fair* (Northcott, Exeter); *Northanger Abbey*, *Amadeus* (Theatre Royal, York); *A Family Affair*, *Double Indemnity*, *Orpheus and Eurydice*, *The Glass Menagerie* (New Wolsey, Ipswich); *Beyond Midnight* (Trestle, Edinburgh Festival); *Rumpelstiltskin*, *Great Expectations* (Unicorn, London); *A Perfect Ganesh*, *The True Life Fiction of Mata Hari* (Palace, Watford); *Richard III*, *Don Juan on Trial*, *The Provok'd Wife*, *Uncle Vanya* (Mercury, Colchester).

His work as a choreographer includes: *The Canterbury Tales* (Northern Broadsides UK Tour); *The Firebird* (Bolton, Octagon); *Talent* (Colchester and Watford); *Little Wolf's Book of Badness* (Hampstead, London); *Duck!* (Unicorn, London).

Alexandra Stafford (*Lighting Designer*)

Alex is delighted to be returning to Nottingham Playhouse to light *The League of Youth*, having previously designed lighting for *The Families of Lockerbie*, *Garage Band* and *Blithe Spirit*.

Other theatre credits include: *The Rivals*, *Proof* (New Vic, Newcastle-under-Lyme); *Mother Came Too*, *Shining City* (Derby LIVE); *Oleanna*, *Much Ado About Nothing* (Buxton Opera House); *Dick Whittington*, *Aladdin*, *Cinderella* (Harrogate); *The Little Mermaid* (Uncontained Arts with Tangere Arts and Buxton Opera House); *A Lady with a Lamp*, *Nicholas Nickleby* for Derby LIVE Youth Theatre; *Cinderella's Sisters* (Red Earth Theatre); *The American Clock*, *Roberto Zucco* (Birmingham School of Acting); *Educating Rita* (University of Derby and Buxton Opera House); *450th Anniversary Son et Lumière* (Repton School); Mahler's *Ruckert Lieder* (Streetwise Opera at Nottingham Council House); *Lady Day at Emerson's Bar and Grill* (New Players, London).

Alex was Head of Lighting at Derby Playhouse (1999–2003). Lighting designs for Derby Playhouse include: *My Dad's Corner Shop*, *Up 'N Under*, *The Blue Room*, *Bouncers*, *Three Viewings*, *A Life in the Theatre*, *A Slice of Saturday Night* and ten traditional pantomimes (1993–2002) for Artistic Director Mark Clements.

Nottingham Playhouse
theatre company

Nottingham Playhouse creates theatre productions large and small: timeless classics, enthralling family shows and adventurous new commissions. It has been one of the United Kingdom's leading producing theatres since its foundation in 1948. Touring work nationally and internationally, the Playhouse remains firmly rooted in its vibrant home city, where its spacious modernist building – fronted by Anish Kapoor's *Sky Mirror* – is one of the region's most popular landmarks.

Under the leadership of Artistic Director Giles Croft and Chief Executive Stephanie Sirr its work has enjoyed ever greater prominence nationally and internationally. Premiered in Nottingham, Steven Berkoff's staging of *On the Waterfront* was presented in Spring 2010 at the Hong Kong Arts Festival, following successful runs in Edinburgh and the West End. At the same time *The Island*, produced as part of the Young Europe exchange programme by the Playhouse's acclaimed Theatre-in-Education company Roundabout, was performed at Det Norske Teatret in Oslo. In 2008 The Playhouse's production of *The Burial at Thebes*, Seamus Heaney's adaptation of *Antigone*, was performed at Spoleto Festival USA (South Carolina) and the International Festival of Arts and Ideas (Connecticut) following its sell-out run at the Barbican.

Other London transfers over the past decade include *Rat Pack Confidential*, *The Railway Children*, *Chicken Soup with Barley* and *Summer and Smoke*. National tours in the same period include *Tracy Beaker Gets Real*, *Old Big 'Ead in The Spirit of the Man*, *Whisky Galore!* and *All Quiet on the Western Front*.

Nottingham Playhouse also enjoys partnerships with many major companies. Recent co-productions include: Steven Berkoff's adaptation of *Oedipus* and Arthur Miller's *The Price* both with Liverpool Playhouse and Everyman; *Arthur & George* with Birmingham Repertory Theatre; *The Changeling* with English Touring Theatre; *Cat on a Hot Tin Roof*, *Mrs Warren's Profession* and *Macbeth*, all with Edinburgh's Royal Lyceum; tours of *A Passage to India*, *War and Peace* and *The Caucasian Chalk Circle* in partnership with Shared Experience; and *The Playboy of the West Indies* with the Tricycle Theatre.

The Playhouse has been an active member of the European Theatre Convention for many years, promoting Nottingham's links with Europe through co-productions and appearances of Nottingham Playhouse's work across the continent. In 2011, Nottingham will play host to neat11, a brand new festival which will see venues across the city celebrate the very best European theatre, dance, music, performance, film and visual art for adults and children. For more information visit **www.neatfestival.co.uk.**

Full information on Nottingham Playhouse's work can be found at **www.nottinghamplayhouse.co.uk**

Artistic Director Giles Croft
Chief Executive Stephanie Sirr
Box Office: 0115 941 9419
Administration: 0115 947 4361

Take a Seat

Dedicate a seat at Nottingham Playhouse and become a permanent part of the theatre that you love.

Contact Nick Lawford on 0115 873 6235 or by emailing nickl@nottinghamplayhouse.co.uk

Nottingham Playhouse would like to thank the following individuals and companies for dedicating a seat:

A20 Kynan Eldridge	L12 Ian Chaplin	N18 Mr Ernest Kemp
D09 Ruth Gardner	L13 Sir Richard Eyre	N19 Mr T Huggon
D10 Mrs J M Connolly	L14 Club Encore	N20 Imperial Tobacco
E8 Simon Ray	L15 The University of	N21 Rae Baker
E12 Peter & Joanne Wright	Nottingham	N22 Lindsay Granger
E13 John Pike	L16 The University of	N23 Roy Boutcher
E14 Hazel Hampton	Nottingham	N24 Dr P Bartlett
E15 Jean & Des Gamlen	L17 Ian Chaplin	N25 Angela Brown
E16 Jean & Des Gamlen	L18 Russell Scanlan	N26 Mr R Gibbons
E17 The Westmoreland Family	L19 Russell Scanlan	N27 Maggie Backhouse
F14 Nottingham Playhouse for	L20 Abigail McKern	O09 Gerard Blair
John Bailey	L21 Mr & Mrs R A Newbery	O10 Design By Tomkins
F15 Mich Stevenson OBE DL	L22 Mr & Mrs R A Newbery	O11 Mrs M Adams
F16 Jan Stevenson	M05 Mr F L Knowles	O12 Simone Lennox-Gordon
G14 Martin Willis	M06 Penny Evans	O13 Brooks and Warman
G15 Zak Horton	M07 The Nottingham Nuffield	Optometrists
G16 Jeanette Spracklen	Hospital	O14 Montague Reynolds
G17 Frances Scott-Lawrence	M08 J Grant	O15 Hart Hambleton plc
G18 Frances Scott-Lawrence	M09 Gill Darvill	O16 Phillip Watts Design
H14 Joan Holden	M10 Browne Jacobson	O17 Dr R Pearce
H15 Petro Zwarycz	M11 Nottingham Evening Post	O18 Dr R Pearce
H16 Karl Alexander Tumour	M12 Nottingham Evening Post	O19 Dr R Pearce
Appeal	M13 Mrs M Durridge	O20 Sid & Carolyn Pritchett
H17 Mrs S Beverton	M14 Miss Judith Platt	O21 Club Encore for Wendy
H18 Nottinghamshire County	M15 Mrs M L Atkinson	Johnson
Council	M16 Mr R V Arnfield	P04 David Tilly
I15 Pearl & Roy Pearson	M17 Mrs J Priestley	P13 Mr M Banks
I16 Pat Salzedo	M18 Miss N Pink	P14 Alan Perrin
I17 Mr & Mrs D W Bostock	M19 Catherine Pitt	P15 The Stoneyholme Trust
I18 Mr & Mrs D W Bostock	M20 Catherine Pitt	P16 Nottingham Playhouse for
J12 Allison Garner	M21 Mrs Irene Atkin	Jean Sands
J15 Harvey Goodman	M22 Mr Brian Livermore	P17 David W Kidd
J16 Mr & Mrs Michael	M23 Cllr C Preston	P18 Phillippe Rogueda
Headland	M24 Mrs E Le Marchant-Brock	P19 Victoria Harrison
J17 Mr & Mrs Michael	M25 Rosie Smith	P20 The A.W. Lymn
Headland	M26 Nottingham Civic Society	Foundation
J18 Mrs E Dougherty	M27 Nottingham Civic Society	Q11 Nottingham Playhouse for
J19 Jenny Farr	M28 Nottingham Civic Society	Jayne Mee
K15 Paul Morris	M29 Nottingham Civic Society	Q12 Mrs S Smart
K16 Ms C Ayre	M30 Nottingham Civic Society	Q13 Mrs S Smart
K17 Mandy Hewitt	N10 Geldards LLP	Q14 A Church
K18 Siobhan McCarthy	N11 Barclays Bank plc	Q15 Marielaine Church
K19 Mrs R Parker	N12 Mrs Maggie Allen	Q16 Marielaine Church
K20 Julia Cooper	N13 Mrs Maggie Allen	Q18 Caroline & David Shutter
K21 Mrs F W Mealor	N14 Mrs Maggie Allen	R13 MR G B Hope
K22 Jane Price	N15 Mrs Maggie Allen	R14 Tony Walker
L04 Tony Wills	N16 Russell Tomlinson	R15 Sue Walker
L11 Barbara Barton (MBE)	N17 Mr Emrys Bryson	S10 J C Spence

Nottingham Playhouse Trust Limited is a registered charity, number 1109342, and is very pleased to be funded by:

We are also very proud to work with the following sponsors: BMIbaby, Cooper Parry, East Midlands Trains, Eversheds, Experian, Harts Nottingham, IKEA, John Lewis, Jurys Inn, NCP, Nottingham Language Academy, Owzat-Cricket, RH Commercial Vehicles, RSM Tenon, The Big Wheel, The Bookcase, Trent Barton and The University of Nottingham.

Inspiration for
every home.

At John Lewis Nottingham we
can turn your ideas into a reality.
Book a furniture consultation with
our Home design advisors for
expert, impartial advice on styles,
colours and all the latest trends.

johnlewis.com/nottingham

Dotty about Patterns
Inspiration for every home

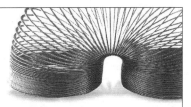

Nottingham Playhouse Staff

Directors
GILES CROFT, Artistic Director
STEPHANIE SIRR, Chief Executive

Administration
Laura Benson, Administration Officer
VALERIE EVANS, Head of Administration
Brenda Frost, PA to Chief Executive & Artistic Director
Robert Hall, ICT Manager

Bea Udeh, Creative Producer

Casting
Sooki McShane CDG Casting Director

Finance
Martin Blee, Finance Manager
Jonathan Child, Finance Officer
Myra Slack, Senior Finance Officer
RACHAEL THOMAS, Head of Finance

Front of House
James Broughton, Performance Fire Warden
Rebecca Dallman, Theatre Manager
Nicola Dawson, Usher
Clare Devine, Usher
Nigel Dickinson, Performance Fire Warden
Wei Dui, Usher
Lucy Eyre, Usher
Heather Galpin, Usher
Kirsty Guest, Usher
Carol Harmer, Usher/Duty FOH Manager
Paul Hawkins, Usher
Laura Hutchinson, Usher
Karen Jones, Usher
Lydia Jones, Usher
Michelle Leek, Usher
Giada Maran, Usher
Beck McGuire, Usher
Livia McLauchlan, House Manager
Clare Moss, Usher
Mufaro Makubika, Usher
Kirk Radcliffe, Performance Fire Warden
Dave Richardson, Usher/Duty FOH Manager
Charlotte Ridley, Usher
Lauren Robinson, Usher
Louise Singleton, Usher
Ollie Smith, Usher/Performance Fire Warden
Joseph Stairs, Usher/Performance Fire Warden
Rose Stapleton, Usher
Richard Swainson, House Manager/Online Content Developer
Bea Wade, Usher
Matt Williams, Usher/Performance Fire Warden

Cleaning & Maintenance
Kevin Bates, Cleaner
Helen Hickling, Cleaner
Annie Lovewell, Head Cleaner
Sheila Sisson, Cleaner
Michael Turton, Maintenance Technician
Maureen Wheat, Cleaner
Paul White, Cleaner

Stage Door
James Broughton, Stage Doorkeeper
Louise Carney, Casual
Nigel Dickenson, Casual
Carol Harmer, Receptionist
Michelle Leek, Receptionist
Geoff Linney, Stage Doorkeeper
John Noton, Stage Doorkeeper
Dave Richardson, Receptionist
Michael Turton, Casual
Susan Yeoman, Receptionist

Marketing & Development
EMMA JONES, Head of Marketing & Communications
Derek Graham, Memberships Manager
Bea Grist, Marketing and Communication Manager
Kayleigh Hunt, Marketing and Communications Assistant
Nick Lawford, Fundraising and Development Manager
Emma O'Neill, Marketing Assistant

Box Office
Adeel Ali, Box Office Assistant
Charlie Cox, Box Office Supervisor
Lauren Harrison, Box Office Assistant
Paul Hawkins, Box Office Assistant
Nadia Lane, Box Office Assistant
Heather Murray, Box Office Assistant
Richard Surgay, Customer Relations Manager
Jeremy Walker, Box Office Assistant

Production
Deborah Reed-Aspley, Assistant Production Manager
JASPER GILBERT, Production Manager

Construction
Mark Bamford, Carpenter
Philip Gunn, Deputy Head of Construction
Julian Smith, Head of Construction

Lighting & Sound
Stephanie Bartle, Lighting & Sound Technician
Drew Baumohl, Deputy Head of Lighting & Sound
Karl Bock, Head of Lighting & Sound
Nick Morris, Lighting & Sound Technician

Paintshop
Sarah Richard, Head of Paintshop
Claire Thompson, Deputy Head of Paintshop

Props
Alex Hatton, Deputy Head of Props
Jane Hyman, Work Placement
Nathan Rose, Head of Props

Stage Management
Kathryn Bainbridge-Wilson, Assistant Stage Manager
Jane Eliot-Webb, Company & Stage Manager
Stuart Lambert, Deputy Stage Manager

Technical
Andy Bartlett, Technical Manager
Andy Nairn, Stage Technician
Jenna Price, Work Experience
Richard Swift, Casual
Tony Topping, Deputy Technical Manager

Wardrobe
Heather Flinders, Wardrobe Assistant
Dani Kidson, Wardrobe Assistant/Dresser
Elaine Pearson, Wardrobe Assistant
Debra Summerfield, Work Experience
Carla Rose, Wardrobe Assistant/Dresser
Helen Tye, Head of Wardrobe
Chrissie Weeds, Freelance Maker

Roundabout
ANDREW BREAKWELL, Director
Kitty Parker, Administrator
Allie Spencer, Education Officer
Sarah Stephenson, Education Officer

THE LEAGUE OF YOUTH

Henrik Ibsen

in a version by Andy Barrett

For Loree, Oliver, Joseph and Isaac

Adapter's Note

The League of Youth is a very long five-act play that presents a couple of obvious difficulties to anyone facing the challenge of writing a version that will hopefully bring the real strengths of the piece to the fore. The first is the parliamentary and local-election system in Norway at the time it was written (1869), and the second is the way that a bill (or promissory note) could be forged and then used by someone who has it in their possession.

I have had a number of long and very useful conversations along the way as I have tried to find a clear path through these questions, particularly with Ola Bo at Det Norske Teatret, and I am reasonably confident that I have managed to bring some clarity to the proceedings.

There have only been two previous published translations, as far as I am aware, one by Ibsen's contemporary William Archer, and another by Peter Watt, both of which I read several times. My source text, however, has been a literal translation by Charlotte Barslund, commissioned by Nottingham Playhouse.

I have also had to cut a couple of characters from the original (there are only so many actors that a theatre can afford to employ, and I'm amazed that I have been given eleven for this production), and this has meant a little bit of re-plotting around the issues of 'partnering up'. We have also doubled up the parts of Ragna and Selma, and Erik and Bastian, but there is of course no need to do this in future productions if the cast is big enough.

Thanks to those colleagues and members of the Playhouse who gave the script its first airing, and to Giles Croft and the cast for their suggestions on the script as we began rehearsals and the obvious errors began to show; and also to Martin Berry for his very careful close-reading. We made a decision between us to refer to Christiana as Oslo in the play, even though this is historically inaccurate.

It's been an absolute joy to be able to bring this play to the UK stage for the first time. As soon as I read it I could see that it was full of Ibsen characters whom I recognised but had never met. I hope that *The League of Youth*, which was Ibsen's first truly successful theatre project, will now get a chance to live again.

Andy Barrett

This text went to press before the end of rehearsals and so may differ slightly from the play as performed.

Characters

STENSGARD, *a lawyer and self-professed radical, orator and pamphleteer; early thirties*

CHAMBERLAIN BRATSBERG, *the owner of the ironworks and the pillar of the community; early sixties*

THORA BRATSBERG, *his daughter; mid-twenties*

ERIK BRATSBERG, *the Chamberlain's son, beginning to dabble in trade and investments; mid-thirties*

SELMA, *his disaffected wife; mid-twenties*

MR MONSEN, *landowner at Storli, a self-made and bluff man; mid-fifties*

BASTIAN MONSEN, *his son, a failed bridge-builder; late twenties*

RAGNA MONSEN, *Monsen's daughter; mid-twenties*

LUNDESTAD, *farmer and Member of Parliament; late fifties*

DR FJELDBO, *an old acquaintance of Stensgard's and also in his early thirties*

DANIEL HEIRE, *an old and bankrupt acquaintance of the Chamberlain; seventies*

ASLAKSEN, *a newspaper printer whose home life has driven him to drink; mid-forties*

MADAM RUNDHOLM, *a rich widow, tradeswoman and owner of the local inn; late thirties*

And LOCAL PEOPLE, MAIDS, SERVANTS, VOTERS, *the* CHAMBERLAIN'S GUESTS

The parts of Erik Bratsberg / Bastian Monsen and of Selma / Ragna Monsen can be doubled.

ACT ONE

It is May 17th. Norwegian Independence Day in an unnamed Norwegian town that is probably based on Ibsen's birthplace, Skien. In other words, a medium-sized town surrounded by woods and forests which bear witness to the thriving timber trade. There is also, in this fictional town, an ironworks that is owned by CHAMBERLAIN BRATSBERG, *the leading aristocrat of the area.*

It is the late nineteenth century and we are in the grounds of BRATSBERG, *who is holding his annual Independence Day party, probably his only concession to any kind of spirit of protest in the town, and presumably grudgingly given. There are festoons in the trees and in the distance we hear music. A small speakers' podium has also been erected.*

On one side of the stage we see the entrance to a marquee, which is the Refreshments Tent. There is a small table outside of this entrance. Elsewhere on the stage is another table, very ornately dressed.

As the curtain is raised we see LUNDESTAD *on the podium, wearing a pair of glasses, which he is peering over. A* CROWD OF PEOPLE – *the ordinary folk of the town who have dressed themselves in their best attire for this annual event – are listening to* LUNDESTAD's *speech.*

LUNDESTAD. And so, my fellow citizens, let me end by raising a toast to freedom on this, our independence day. A freedom that we have inherited from our fathers and which, through careful tending, we will pass on in fine shape to our sons.

ALL. To freedom!

The CROWD *lift their glasses as a group of people come through them;* MONSEN, *the biggest landowner of the rapidly developing merchant class who has made good*

without a classical education; BASTIAN, *his son;*
ASLAKSEN *the printer, a weasel-like man; and*
STENSGARD, *a new arrival to the town. This is a man who
is keen on making a good impression with the way he dresses.*

MONSEN. The same old speech every year. I almost think he's
beginning to believe it.

ASLAKSEN. It makes my job easy.

They sit down at the ornately dressed table.

MONSEN. Well, Mr Stensgard, let us have a proper talk about
politics.

STENSGARD. Indeed. This is a day on which serious matters
should be discussed by serious men.

MONSEN. Excellent!

STENSGARD. And will Ragna be joining us at some point?

MONSEN. Politics, Mr Stensgard! Politics!

LUNDESTAD *now approaches them.*

LUNDESTAD. Gentlemen, I am afraid that this table is reserved.

STENSGARD. Who for?

LUNDESTAD. The Chamberlain's party.

STENSGARD. But none of them are here.

LUNDESTAD. They will be arriving soon.

STENSGARD. I'm sure they won't mind sitting elsewhere.

LUNDESTAD. No. This is where the Chamberlain will sit.

There is a moment as LUNDESTAD *and* STENSGARD *eye
each other.*

MONSEN. Oh, come on, man! These flowers would make
Aslaksen sneeze all over us anyway. Over there, look. That'll
do the job nicely.

MONSEN *gets up to move to the other table and*
STENSGARD, *reluctantly, does so as well.*

LUNDESTAD. Thank you. And my apologies for any confusion that may have been caused.

MONSEN. There is no confusion, Lundestad. Chamberlain Bratsberg is to have pride of place as always.

LUNDESTAD. We are on his land.

MONSEN. Yes, yes! Now can you arrange for some champagne to be brought over to us, please?

LUNDESTAD. Your custom in the Refreshments Tent will be most welcome.

LUNDESTAD *exits into the Refreshments Tent.*

MONSEN. Bastian, go and fetch us four bottles of the very best champagne. (*To the world at large, i.e.* LUNDESTAD.) Tell them that Monsen is paying and business is booming!

BASTIAN *enters the tent.* MONSEN, STENSGARD *and* ASLAKSEN *sit down at the other table.*

You see, we all have our place here, Stensgard. And by Christ aren't we made to know it.

STENSGARD. Is there nobody who is willing to stand up to this?

MONSEN. God no! Everyone's much too set in their ways to even think about kicking up a stink. But your arrival in our district is just what we need. I may not be the most educated man but that does not stop me from keeping a careful eye on the way that the world is moving outside of our little community. And you have made your mark, all right. Oh yes, we've read about you, Mr Stensgard. There are one or two of us who dare to get our hands on the progressive papers. Whatever our neighbours might think. One or two who understand that these are exciting times, ripe for change.

MADAM RUNDHOLM *enters with the champagne, followed by* BASTIAN.

Ah, here it comes!

MADAM RUNDHOLM. Good evening, gentlemen.

MADAM RUNDHOLM *begins to pour the champagne.*

MONSEN. Leave that to Bastian, Madam Rundholm. He needs to earn his keep. Maybe you can find him a job in the champagne trade? There's good money to be made with this stuff.

MADAM RUNDHOLM. I think I'm doing all right as I am, thank you, Mr Monsen.

MADAM RUNDHOLM *exits.* ASLAKSEN *goes to drink but* MONSEN *glares at him and he puts the glass down.*

MONSEN. A toast then. To Mr Stensgard. And may I say what an honour it is for a simple man like me to be able to count you as a friend.

ASLAKSEN. Hear, hear!

MONSEN *and* ASLAKSEN *down their champagne.* MONSEN *indicates to* BASTIAN *to pour some more. He tops up all of the glasses even though* STENSGARD *indicates that he does not want any more put into his glass.*

MONSEN. Of course it's not really Bratsberg that holds things up here, but Lundestad. Making sure that the Chamberlain's best interests are served.

STENSGARD. I heard someone say that he thought of himself as a liberal.

MONSEN. Lundestad? Oh, maybe when he was younger, but now he is as conservative as the rest of them. I tell you, between the Chamberlain and our farmer friend they've got the whole thing sewn up.

STENSGARD. But surely there must be some way of putting an end to this.

BASTIAN. Yes! You're right.

ASLAKSEN. And you are the man.

STENSGARD. But I am new here. What can I do?

MONSEN. We know that you have a talent for advancing the most current thinking.

ASLAKSEN. And my paper would be at your disposal.

MONSEN. If you ever felt the urge to put pen to paper.

BASTIAN. And with the local election only a few days away…

MONSEN.…this would be an ideal time for those who support progress to let their voices be heard.

STENSGARD. I see.

ASLAKSEN. Mr Monsen already has the support of most of the more forward-thinking members of our community.

MONSEN. Those who understand that money must be made rather than passed down on the top of a coffin. And the one thing that our meetings at Storli lack is someone who can put things into words. It's so damned difficult.

BASTIAN. And if he was to be victorious in the local election then he would have a chance of going on to sit in Parliament. Like Lundestad.

STENSGARD. Well, I am sure that I could contribute.

MONSEN. Another glass, Bastian.

STENSGARD. No I'm fine, really.

MONSEN. Nonsense.

BASTIAN *pours the champagne.*

To Mr Stensgard. And his relentless support for new ideas.

The table say 'Hear! Hear!' and down their champagne.

And may he kick some sense into us all. Some more than others, of course.

MONSEN *nods at* BASTIAN, *who pours more champagne.*

STENSGARD. No, please. I really have had enough.

MONSEN. Come on, man! Another glass. To toast our pact.

They drink again. Again ASLAKSEN *and* MONSEN *knock back their champagne whilst* STENSGARD *has a little sip.* DANIEL HEIRE *enters from the tent. He is a wizened little man who has obviously seen better days, and is short-sighted. He peers at the table and approaches.*

Look who's coming.

ASLAKSEN. Always managing to find a way to stick his nose in.

HEIRE. Good evening, gentlemen.

MONSEN. Would you like to join us, Daniel?

HEIRE. Thank you.

He sits down.

Ah, champagne.

MONSEN. May we offer you a glass?

HEIRE. Well, I'm not sure if I should. But then of course I was always told it's rude to turn down an offer. Just the one. For now.

BASTIAN *pours a glass for* HEIRE. MONSEN *indicates that* BASTIAN *is to top up his glass as well, which he does. As he is doing this,* ASLAKSEN *downs his glass and so* BASTIAN *tops that up and then pours more champagne in* STENSGARD'*s glass, who again tries to prevent this from happening.*

And who is this?

MONSEN. Our new arrival.

HEIRE. Ah, the lawyer Mr Stensgard, who stands firmly for the forces of progress!

MONSEN. This is the fellow. And this is Daniel Heire…

BASTIAN.…the capitalist.

HEIRE. Ex-capitalist. Through no fault of my own. Not that I want to cast blame, good gracious no.

MONSEN. Good. Then let's drink up before it all goes flat.

HEIRE. Even when we are sitting in his grounds.

There is a sense from those around the table that they have heard this before. STENSGARD *is however slightly surprised by what he has heard.*

Yes, that's right, Mr Stensgard. Our respectable host is more than he seems. Or should I say less. Twenty years ago I had money coming out of my ears. Have you heard of my father?

STENSGARD. No I do not think th…

HEIRE.…he was a shipowner who made his fortune and passed it on to me. He knew how to enjoy his money, like Monsen here. As did I. But there is a difference. I have made it my passion to promote young talent. Always.

ASLAKSEN. I think that I should go and see who else is here. The circulation is always the highest after today's event. Excuse me, gentlemen.

ASLAKSEN *exits into the Refreshments Tent.*

HEIRE. He is one of them. I paid for him to study for a whole year. Not that I get any thanks for my troubles.

STENSGARD. Aslaksen went to university? He doesn't seem the type.

HEIRE. He did. And what was the point? A waste of potential, just like young Monsen here. And a tippler too.

He looks up to indicate to BASTIAN *that his glass is empty.* BASTIAN *pours him one and* HEIRE *begins to drink.* MONSEN *indicates to* HEIRE *that he should continue his story.*

So my father found himself at the very top of the tree just as our Chamberlain's father began to struggle. Bad investments, poor judgement, the usual thing. And he had to sell off some land. Which my father bought.

STENSGARD. Was Bratsberg's father a Chamberlain too?

MONSEN. Damn right he was.

BASTIAN. Everything is inherited here.

HEIRE. And in time the land passes to me and I make all kinds of improvements, chopping down all the dead wood. Until, out of nowhere, this Chamberlain who parades himself as the model of civic virtue manages to bamboozle everyone. To have the sale reversed and the deeds passed back to him.

STENSGARD. But surely you could have prevented that from happening?

HEIRE. I tried, I did, but he started stamping his feet and pointing to a number of apparent minor flaws in the original contract. And suddenly it was as though I was in the wrong. Can you believe such an injustice? Although I did have a temporary cash-flow problem which unfortunately turned out to be permanent. And so I had no alternative but to accept the meagre compensation payment that I was awarded.

MONSEN. And you can't blame a man for trying to get hold of capital when he needs it. This new world demands that we all make money but you try finding some to get started with. Those who have it keep it for themselves, that's for sure.

HEIRE. Absolutely. Look at when they wanted a manager for the savings bank here. Mr Monsen threw his hat into the ring but oh no they didn't want someone like him. Someone who understands how capital works. They wanted someone who would keep things tight.

MONSEN (*indicating the empty table*). They hold us back! In every way they hold us back!

BASTIAN. Who gets the contracts for any civil-engineering work round here? I went to university. I have the qualifications.

HEIRE. And when you did build a bridge, Bastian, it fell down.

BASTIAN. It was a simple mistake that anyone could have made.

HEIRE. Well, I am sure Mr Stensgard has heard enough. We don't want to overstep the mark. Otherwise he may feel the need to make our views known to the Chamberlain on his next visit there.

BASTIAN. What do you mean?

HEIRE. I'm sorry. Have I put my foot in it?

MONSEN. Have you paid a visit to the Chamberlain?

STENSGARD. I have not.

HEIRE. I must have been mistaken. Please accept my apologies. Although I'm sure I saw you heading that way in the most beautiful coat.

STENSGARD. Official business; nothing personal.

BASTIAN. So you have.

HEIRE. Don't worry, he didn't let him in.

STENSGARD. You seem to know a lot, Mr Heire.

HEIRE. And how must that have made you feel, Mr Stensgard? You, a new and distinguished member of our community, not being welcomed into the Chamberlain's house. The Chamberlain who puffs himself up and announces to everyone that 'my door is always open to decent people'.

STENSGARD. He says that?

HEIRE. He does. But do not worry; Mr Monsen has never been welcome either. Although I don't understand what it is he has against you? Unless someone has told him of your inclinations. He does like to know everything that is going on. And I have heard that he has described you as... no, no I have gone too far.

HEIRE's *glass is empty and* MONSEN *fills it for him. The bottle is now empty.* MONSEN *hands it to* BASTIAN *and indicates to him that he is to go the Refreshments Tent.* BASTIAN *exits.*

STENSGARD. Tell me.

HEIRE. It would not be polite. (*Takes a drink of champagne.*)
As an empty windbag and an opportunist.

STENSGARD. And you heard this?

HEIRE. If I had been present then of course I would have come
to your defence. No man deserves to be written off so easily.

STENSGARD. How dare he!

HEIRE. But we are jumping to conclusions. And intelligent
men must never do such a thing. I'm sure you can ask him
for an explanation tomorrow.

STENSGARD. What are you on about?

HEIRE. The luncheon party that he holds every year after
Independence Day. All men of substance are invited to
discuss matters of local and national importance. Surely you
have been invited?

LUNDESTAD *takes to the podium once again as*
BRATSBERG, *his daughter* THORA, *and* DR FJELDBO
enter.

MONSEN. Here they come. Will you please excuse me, Mr
Stensgard? This is one of those days where business and
pleasure go hand in hand. And I can't stand the thought of
hearing Lundestad banging on again.

STENSGARD. Of course.

MONSEN. Let us begin work together immediately. The
election is almost upon us.

STENSGARD. And I must and will do all I can to support you.

MONSEN. Good.

MONSEN *exits as* LUNDESTAD *begins:*

LUNDESTAD. My friends, if I may please say a few more
words.

STENSGARD *now stands up and begins to shout:*

STENSGARD. I would like to be heard as well, Mr Lundestad!

LUNDESTAD. Maybe when I have finished.

STENSGARD. No – now!

LUNDESTAD. Patience, Mr Stensgard. You are new here and must learn the proper etiquette.

STENSGARD sits down, absolutely fuming.

Ladies and gentlemen, we have toasted our independence but now let us toast the man who has been such a generous provider for our community for as long as we can remember. A man whose door is never closed to any decent citizen amongst us. To Chamberlain Bratsberg and his family!

ALL. Chamberlain Bratsberg and his family!

Applause as BRATSBERG is surrounded by the CROWD; shaking of hands, etc.

STENSGARD. And may I speak now?

LUNDESTAD. The podium is yours.

STENSGARD leaps onto the table.

STENSGARD. I make my own podium!

There is gathering interest in STENSGARD. BRATSBERG turns to FJELDBO:

BRATSBERG. Who is this upstart?

FJELDBO. Mr Stensgard, the lawyer.

BRATSBERG. The one that Lundestad has been talking about?

FJELDBO. Yes.

ERIK BRATSBERG enters with his wife SELMA.

BRATSBERG. Erik and Selma, excellent. But she really should be wearing a shawl.

BRATSBERG moves off towards ERIK and SELMA and they begin to converse as STENSGARD begins his speech.

STENSGARD. Brothers – and sisters – please may I have your attention for one moment on this day of celebration. This day when we mark the moment our country began to emerge as an independent nation. I know that I am new amongst you, having only been here for six months now, and yet I know also that your generosity of spirit will allow me to be honest about what I see before me.

LUNDESTAD. I hope your contribution will be brief, Mr Stensgard.

STENSGARD. Ah, there we have it, my friends. There we have it. Yes, you may speak but only until we have decided that we have heard enough!

There is growing interest from the CROWD. MONSEN *and* ASLAKSEN *enter from the Refreshments Tent.*

But why should this be? Why should we stand here on this day of all days and let them tell us how the world is to be run; how our lives are to be led; how we must climb out of our cots in deference and clamber back into our graves in deference still. Surely we can see that this world around us is changing? And yet they do not want this. They do not want to accept that their power may be under threat. (*Beginning to get caught up in his own rhetoric now.*) Can you not smell it? The musty stench of tradition. Can you not hear it? The cries of liberty being smothered by the hoary hands of privilege! Well – enough is enough!

The CROWD *is beginning to get excited.*

Look at this gathering. This barren fête. It is as though we are all marching to a funeral. Yet this is the time of growth! The time when new shoots push through the earth, hungry to see the light. Oh, my friends, my friends and comrades, this should be a world, a joyful world, of hope and opportunity, not one that is bound by the ghosts of the past.

At this there is some applause which catches BRATSBERG's *attention, as* ERIK *and* SELMA *exit.*

BRATSBERG. What is he actually talking about, doctor?

FJELDBO. He is just caught up in the moment, Chamberlain. And he has drunk rather a lot of champagne.

STENSGARD. And we can make that world, we can discover it if we dare to be bold. If we dare to grab hold of the reins even though the horses that pull us may be difficult to control and our hands end up bloodied and sore.

BRATSBERG. He seems to be getting the crowd very worked up.

STENSGARD. I do not know which of you will join me. But unlike some I will not shut my door to you.

THORA *and* FJELDBO *make a decision between them that the sensible option is for* BRATSBERG *to leave before he realises what is going on.*

THORA. Come on, Father. I insist. We have many people to thank.

STENSGARD. And between us we will be heard! The voice of liberty and progress will drown out the rasping wheeze of greed and privilege.

FJELDBO *quickly cuts in so that* BRATSBERG *does not hear the last word 'privilege'.*

FJELDBO. Ah! He is declaiming the greed that is infecting our community, Chamberlain. Obviously an attack on Monsen and his like.

There is now more applause.

BRATSBERG. Well, somebody had to do it. Good for him.

THORA. Come on, Father. In case you are seen to be siding with such aggressive views. You may disagree with everything Monsen stands for but he is a very influential man.

BRATSBERG. You're right; as usual. She is the soul of discretion, doctor. Come on. Did we invite him to the luncheon tomorrow?

THORA *exits with* BRATSBERG, *whispering a 'thank you' to* FJELDBO.

STENSGARD. Oh, my friends, we will come together as one! Those who are strong in spirit; who embrace idealism on this day which calls out for heroes to make their stand. I am here for you. And I say let us create, this very day, this very hour, our movement, our league, our League of Youth!

The CROWD *cheers. There is a real sense of excitement.*

ASLAKSEN. Into the Refreshment Tent! I will gather paper and pens.

STENSGARD. We can change the world, my friends! Right here! Right now!

The CROWD *pick up* STENSGARD *and carry him into the tent. As they do this* LUNDESTAD *comes over to* FJELDBO.

LUNDESTAD. Well, well, that was unexpected.

FJELDBO. Just a moment of excitement and nothing more. I'm sure it'll all come to nothing, like most things.

LUNDESTAD. I don't know, doctor, I don't know. And with the local election so near it is bound to have some influence.

FJELDBO. You seem a little concerned.

LUNDESTAD. One shouldn't be afraid of competition.

FJELDBO. He is a man who wants to get ahead.

LUNDESTAD. Don't we all want to get ahead when we are younger?

HEIRE (*who has been watching the proceedings throughout*) *comes forward as there is a big cheer from the tent.*

Maybe I should go and see what is happening.

HEIRE. And form the official opposition.

LUNDESTAD *enters the Refreshments Tent.*

Not too much heckling now! This is wonderful; don't you agree, doctor? I imagine our old farmer Lundestad is feeling rather rattled.

FJELDBO. Why is it of such interest to you?

HEIRE. Can't you see the fun that we're to have? How the great and the good are going to have to hold onto their hats. Not that I'm interested personally, of course. It is all the same to me whether the pig eats the dog, or the dog the pig.

From inside the tent there is a chant of 'Long live Stensgard! Long live Stensgard!'

Are you not coming in?

FJELDBO. No.

HEIRE *enters the tent as* BASTIAN *comes out of it.*

BASTIAN. I was the first to sign.

FJELDBO. Well done.

BASTIAN. What a man he is. I feel so moved, so passionate. I must do something!

FJELDBO. And what is that?

BASTIAN. I will go down to the dance hall and pick a fight.

There is another cheer from the tent. BASTIAN *looks round, pumps up his fists and exits, as* STENSGARD *enters from the tent.*

STENSGARD. My dear Fjeldbo.

FJELDBO. You seem to have made quite an impression. What is happening in there now?

STENSGARD. Aslaksen is dealing with the formalities of the League's formation.

FJELDBO. And now that you have announced your arrival in such a fashion, what position will you be offered to accommodate and calm you? A seat on the council perhaps?

STENSGARD. Why do you talk to me in this way?

FJELDBO. Or maybe you can become the bank manager.

STENSGARD. Fjeldbo! I feel as though you misunderstand me. Come. Let us be friends as before.

STENSGARD *holds out his hand to* FJELDBO.

I promise that I will rise to this challenge, Fjeldbo. That I will repay the trust that has been put in me.

FJELDBO. Then let me begin again and congratulate you.

FJELDBO *takes* STENSGARD*'s hand.*

STENSGARD. Thank you! Let us be faithful and true to each other so that we can be as close as we were.

There. You see. Oh, I am so happy, my friend. I knew, I always knew... But now! Is it not a blessing to have this talent? To be able to gather them in the palm of my hand, to carry them away with my vision, to make them realise what is possible. I feel as though I want to embrace all of mankind, to gather them up in my arms and beg for their forgiveness because I have been given such ability, because I have been given so much more than them.

FJELDBO. Then we have both been given reason for thanks this evening.

STENSGARD. Yes, you have found me again!

FJELDBO *looks at* STENSGARD *with a mixture of affection and confusion. He knows that* STENSGARD *does not understand what he means, but he is not going to tell him that he and* THORA *have, that evening, betrothed themselves to each other.*

What a lovely night. The music floats out over the meadows and it is so still here in the valley. Our lives are beginning afresh at this very hour, my friend.

FJELDBO. And what are you to do next? How are you to build on your triumph?

STENSGARD. I must be the voice that raises a hurricane.

FJELDBO. Listen, my friend; you must not get carried away.

STENSGARD. This is only the first step. All movements have to begin somewhere. All leaders have to find the battleground on which they will stake their claim.

FJELDBO. But can you not see that maybe you are being manipulated? That Monsen and his ridiculous followers have turned you against a decent man.

STENSGARD. Nonsense. Mr Monsen has welcomed me into his house, unlike some. I can see that he is able, that he has insight into public matters.

FJELDBO. You mean he has read all of the articles that you have written in the papers and conveniently agrees with every single one of them.

STENSGARD. Why this bitterness? Why do you always see the worst in people? I am ambitious, Fjeldbo. You know that. But you have never understood what this feeling is like. This urge.

FJELDBO. I have never tried to fool myself by passionate outbursts that have no real connection with the life that I am leading.

STENSGARD. You have drifted through everything.

FJELDBO. And I have enjoyed it.

There is a moment of acceptance and reconciliation.

STENSGARD. You heard of my situation in Oslo? How I had to break off my engagement?

FJELDBO. Yes.

STENSGARD. It was best for everyone. And there was no question I had to leave.

FJELDBO. And so you decided to come here.

STENSGARD. Why not?

FJELDBO. Indeed.

STENSGARD. Look, can I ask you something?

FJELDBO. Of course.

STENSGARD. Do you know Ragna?

FJELDBO. Monsen's daughter?

STENSGARD. Yes.

FJELDBO. I do. She sometimes visits Thora... the Chamberlain's daughter.

STENSGARD. And what do you think of her?

FJELDBO. From what I have seen and heard, she is a lovely young woman.

STENSGARD. Yes.

FJELDBO. And?

STENSGARD. Need I say more.

FJELDBO. Then that is wonderful news. And believe me, you should concentrate on this. On the winning of her. Not these stupid political battles.

STENSGARD. I do not see how this success can harm my chances at all.

From inside the tent we hear a shout of 'To Stensgard!'

Listen. Can you hear my name? They are drinking to me. It is real now. It has begun and they need me to drive things forward.

RAGNA MONSEN *and* THORA *now enter.*

Good evening, ladies. Ragna.

RAGNA. Good evening, Mr Stensgard. You seem to have created quite a stir.

THORA. Let us hope that they do not all get too carried away.

FJELDBO. May I introduce Miss Thora Bratsberg.

STENSGARD. I am honoured.

THORA. I have been asked to deliver a letter to you, sir. From my father.

She hands STENSGARD *the letter.*

STENSGARD. Thank you. I look forward to reading it.

FJELDBO. May I escort you home?

THORA. No thank you. Ragna and I have much to discuss. And I would not want to break up the conversation of friends.

THORA *gives* FJELDBO *a small, disparaging look.*

FJELDBO. Of course.

STENSGARD. Goodnight, ladies.

RAGNA. Goodnight.

RAGNA *and* THORA *exit.* STENSGARD *watches them go and as soon as they are out of sight he tears open the letter and reads it.*

FJELDBO. So why does the Chamberlain write to you?

STENSGARD *starts to laugh.*

What is it?

STENSGARD. This decent man you talk of, Fjeldbo, is pathetic. And you can tell him, and everyone else, that I said so.

The CROWD *appears from the tent.* LUNDESTAD *is holding* STENSGARD*'s hat,* ASLAKSEN *a bowl of punch,* MONSEN *is also with them.*

LUNDESTAD. You forgot your hat, Mr Stensgard.

STENSGARD. Thank you.

ASLAKSEN. And here's some punch. Drink up! Every man of spirit has pledged themselves to your League!

MONSEN. And tomorrow we will all meet at Storli where Mr Stensgard is to launch the manifesto and has promised to speak of the election.

There is a cheer from the CROWD.

STENSGARD. Does it have to be tomorrow?

MONSEN. They're all baying for it. And I'll make sure there's one hell of a spread.

STENSGARD. Well, we'll see, though I think tomorrow may be a bit of a problem. The day after would be better, I think. Yes, much better. Goodnight, gentlemen. The old ways are cracking open! And the roar of progress will come galloping through. On horses driven by the common man!

MONSEN. Let us accompany you home. A guard of honour!

STENSGARD. No, really, I am fine, thank you. Though if you must. Are you coming, Fjeldbo?

FJELDBO. No.

STENSGARD. Well, goodnight. And perhaps I was a bit harsh with the Chamberlain. Maybe it is best if you don't mention what I said to anyone for now.

ASLAKSEN *grabs his arm.*

ASLAKSEN. Come on, man! This is your moment. Music!

Music begins as STENSGARD *is surrounded by the* CROWD *and herded off of the stage.* FJELDBO *and* LUNDESTAD *are left behind.*

LUNDESTAD. What a strange evening it has been.

FJELDBO. And where are you going now, Mr Lundestad? There is nothing left to do here.

LUNDESTAD. Me? I'm going home to bed.

And now the music cross-fades as the scene does too. The raucous folk-singing and fiddle-playing that accompanied STENSGARD *on his triumphant exit turns into the gentle strains of a chamber orchestra. The stage is transformed into the conservatory of* BRATSBERG*'s house. It is the next day and the excited conversation of the members of the League of Youth has now become the polite chit-chat of the respectable members of society who have been invited to* BRATSBERG*'s annual post-Independence Day dinner.*

We see several GUESTS *cross the stage to enter the dining room, which is off the conservatory, as is the garden. A* MAID *crosses with a tray of drinks.*

ASLAKSEN *is sitting on a chair on his own, waiting.* FJELDBO *enters from the garden.*

FJELDBO. Aslaksen. I didn't expect to see you here.

ASLAKSEN. I'm waiting for someone. And why are you so late?

FJELDBO. There was a patient I had to see. And how is your family?

ASLAKSEN. My wife is in bed as usual, hacking all over the sheets, and my eldest son continues to be a cripple. So what is the point of talking about it?

FJELDBO. You've been drinking.

ASLAKSEN. So are they. In there.

FJELDBO. That's different.

ASLAKSEN. Is it?

FJELDBO. You may have a point. But we all have to live with what we are given.

ASLAKSEN. I used to sit in there too. When Daniel Heire took me from the printing business and paid for me to study. I was well-dressed and well-read and carefully picked up my knife and fork as the gravy boat was laid on the table. And then Chamberlain Bratsberg decides to ruin my patron and that was the end of that.

FJELDBO. Daniel Heire ruined himself. And you had your trade to return to.

ASLAKSEN. But how do you think it felt to me then? When I started out I was proud to be a printer, but ever since it has reeked of failure. And once you have been shown from the table, once you have been told that you cannot mix with these men, then your failure trails around with you for the rest of your life. Like a bad smell. And every morning it's still there, however wide you open the windows. Yes, doctor, I have been drinking.

FJELDBO. We must all try and escape the clutches of envy.

And at this moment, from the dining room, we hear a small eruption of laughter as the GUESTS *leave to enter into the garden.* STENSGARD *is at the front of the gathering, and has* THORA *on his left arm and* SELMA *on his right.*

STENSGARD. Well, I am a stranger here, so you ladies must tell me where to escort you.

SELMA. Out into the open; you must see the garden.

STENSGARD. And I am sure that it too will be delightful.

STENSGARD, SELMA *and* THORA *have now exited into the garden as the other* GUESTS *continue to pass through.*

FJELDBO. What's Stensgard doing here?

ASLAKSEN. Keeping me waiting.

FJELDBO. And why do you need to see him?

ASLAKSEN. For the article, about the League of Youth.

FJELDBO. I do not think this is the time or the place to talk about that.

ASLAKSEN. I am a printer. My paper will be part of this movement. They will see, in there, that I can still be heard in this town.

FJELDBO. I will find him and send him to you. And I suggest that in the meantime you go home; for your own sake.

FJELDBO *enters the garden.* ASLAKSEN *sits and listens to the conversation and music for a moment before deciding to go. He shakes his head, stands up and is about to put his coat on when* LUNDESTAD *enters from the dining room.*

LUNDESTAD. What are you doing here?

ASLAKSEN. Leaving. And why are you bothered about me? Surely there are others here who are more of a threat?

LUNDESTAD. I see no reason why he shouldn't have been invited.

ASLAKSEN. Perhaps the Chamberlain is afraid of him.

LUNDESTAD. I doubt it. Cautious maybe.

ASLAKSEN. And how confident are you in that opinion, Lundestad? We all know the people who you stand up for. But will they still stand up for you?

LUNDESTAD. Do not worry about me. I am able to look after myself.

ASLAKSEN. But you don't really belong, do you? And when the time comes and you have served your purpose then they will put you down like an old dog. Are they serving drinks in the garden?

LUNDESTAD. Maybe you should leave.

ASLAKSEN. Why does everyone keep telling me that?

ASLAKSEN *heads for the door to the garden, his coat still sitting on the chair, as* STENSGARD *enters with* SELMA *from the garden.*

Ah, there you are.

STENSGARD. Not now!

ASLAKSEN *is about to continue the conversation but realises that nobody wants to see him and goes into the garden.*

LUNDESTAD. Did you enjoy the meal, Mr Stensgard?

STENSGARD. Yes I did, thank you.

LUNDESTAD. The food here is always perfect.

STENSGARD. I can imagine that one's own table can seem quite ruined in comparison.

LUNDESTAD. Yes. Well, maybe we can share a cigar later. Excuse me.

LUNDESTAD *goes out into the garden.*

STENSGARD. You are right; it is such a beautiful view.

SELMA. I love coming here.

STENSGARD. You do not live in the house then?

SELMA. No. My husband and I have our own house in town.

STENSGARD. And do you have a family?

SELMA. We fairytale princesses don't have families.

STENSGARD. So you are a princess?

SELMA. Of all the sunken castles where enchantment happens on a Midsummer Eve. Doctor Fjeldbo thinks that it must be the most perfect life, but let me tell you...

ERIK *enters from the dining room.*

ERIK. Ah, I have found my little wife at last.

SELMA. Your wife is enjoying the company of Mr Stensgard. I felt a little cold and decided to tell him my life story.

ERIK. And what part do I play in it?

SELMA. You are the prince, of course. There is always a prince and the prince lifts a spell and everything is well again. And then we all celebrate and the fairytale ends.

ERIK (*putting his arms round* SELMA). But don't forget that the princess goes on to become the queen.

SELMA. Only if they go abroad to a foreign kingdom.

STENSGARD. And what kind of kingdom would you like to go to?

SELMA. Oh, I would not get to have a say, Mr Stensgard, not at all. But it would be somewhere with a temperate climate. That is what my husband prefers.

THORA *enters from the dining room.*

Here she is! I hope you have been well diagnosed.

THORA. What do you mean?

SELMA. With all the attention you are letting the doctor pay to you, I can only presume you have the most terrible illness. And look how she flushes! Perhaps you should call him again.

BRATSBERG *enters from the dining room.*

BRATSBERG. Ah, my dear ladies, getting to know our new arrival. It appears as though he has charmed all of you tonight.

SELMA. Well, it would be rude for us to take him all for ourselves then. Come on, Erik, let us leave these men to make their plans. And I'm sure that Thora and I have much to discuss.

THORA, ERIK *and* SELMA *exit into the garden.*

BRATSBERG. Selma is an exquisite creature.

STENSGARD. Yes.

BRATSBERG. I have to thank Daniel Heire for bringing her into our lives. A child prodigy, musically brilliant, but an orphan. It was he that looked after her until his situation... changed. But by then she was welcome in all of the best circles. And met my son.

STENSGARD. You speak fondly of Mr Heire.

BRATSBERG. We have known each other since years back. And have kept running into each other ever since.

STENSGARD. Chamberlain, it was terribly wrong of me to be so aggressive yesterday.

BRATSBERG. Yes, that may be so, but your intention was good, I think most people will agree with that. There is etiquette, of course, ways in which points should be put across, but sometimes things simply have to be said. So we can perhaps overlook the tone of your oratory on this occasion.

STENSGARD. That is most gracious of you.

BRATSBERG. And now that I have finally made your acquaintance, I hope that you will be able to come to me whenever you have anything on your mind. We all want what is best for our community. That is my duty after all.

STENSGARD. And I could speak frankly to you? Man to man?

BRATSBERG. Of course. Look, I am not unaware of certain trends of thought. But I am old and it is against my nature to embrace any calls for reform. And anyway, it would be pointless because I simply do not understand them. I do what is expected of me, my duty, as a man who has been given the title of Chamberlain by the King; and I believe I have done it to the best of my abilities. My ironworks put food in the mouths of families here, I have been beneficent with my wealth, and our community is, I am sure you will agree, a peaceful and happy one.

STENSGARD. There are those who see things in a slightly different light.

BRATSBERG. Well, let them. I try not to get involved in public affairs, at least not openly. I don't much like the way that one has to conduct oneself in that world. Whereas you, well, you have the skills necessary for such... activities. So it would seem to make sense if we could work together.

STENSGARD. I am sure that we could be of assistance to each other.

BRATSBERG. We are agreed then.

STENSGARD. Thank you, Chamberlain. Thank you.

HEIRE *enters from the garden.*

BRATSBERG. Daniel! We were just talking about you.

HEIRE. Well, there's plenty of talk out there.

BRATSBERG. What do you mean?

HEIRE. Lundestad has made a speech. It seems to be catching on.

BRATSBERG. I asked him to set up the games table.

HEIRE. Oh, it's all going to add to the fun, that's for sure.

STENSGARD. What did he say?

HEIRE. He has declared that he is soon to retire from public life. That he intends to spend more time with his family.

BRATSBERG. What is the meaning of this?

HEIRE. Surely it's not that difficult to guess.

BRATSBERG. This is a serious matter for our community. Excuse me, gentlemen, I must go and talk to the man.

BRATSBERG *begins to exit as* FJELDBO *enters from the garden.*

FJELDBO. Ah, Chamberlain, I was hoping that I might get a moment to…

BRATSBERG. Not now, man! Not now!

BRATSBERG *exits into the garden.*

HEIRE. Oh, how wonderful this all is. Who would have thought anything could prise our old farmer from Parliament.

STENSGARD. But why has he done it?

HEIRE. It is the League of Youth! It's beginning to pump some new air through the place like a pair of Bratsberg's bellows.

STENSGARD. Do you think so?

HEIRE. Of course. I'm off to see Monsen to tell him the news.

FJELDBO. And why do you want to do that?

HEIRE. To add to the excitement. If Lundestad stands aside maybe Monsen really will get to sit in Parliament.

HEIRE *exits into the garden.*

STENSGARD. Well, I wasn't expecting this.

FJELDBO. It's not the only thing that is unexpected this evening.

STENSGARD. Why, what else has happened?

FJELDBO. I mean your presence here.

STENSGARD. I was invited.

FJELDBO. I know. Last night. After your outburst.

STENSGARD. So?

FJELDBO. How could you possibly accept after saying what you did?

STENSGARD. What was I supposed to do? Appear insolent and turn down a request for my company? I have no desire to insult these people.

FJELDBO. You managed to in your speech.

STENSGARD. No, you're mistaken. Absolutely mistaken. I was quite clearly attacking principles, not people. There's a world of difference. You obviously weren't paying close enough attention.

FJELDBO. And why do you think the Chamberlain has invited you here tonight?

STENSGARD. Surely that is obvious.

FJELDBO. You think he is afraid of you? That you are a real threat?

STENSGARD. Perhaps.

FJELDBO. You wouldn't consider that it could be something else?

STENSGARD. Like what?

FJELDBO. That maybe he did not fully understand the purpose of your attack.

STENSGARD. What I said was clear. But he is man enough to have seen the value of what lay behind my words.

FJELDBO. You are sure of this?

STENSGARD. Absolutely. And we have made an agreement Fjeldbo, the Chamberlain and I, an agreement that we are to work together for the common good.

FJELDBO. Together?

STENSGARD. We each have our roles to play.

FJELDBO. I am not sure how such a proposal will be received by Monsen and his people at Storli.

STENSGARD. I have my own power base, the League of Youth.

FJELDBO. Full of baying young radicals.

STENSGARD. Who require me to put their principles into practice.

FJELDBO. And your hopes of a relationship with Ragna? I thought that your presence at Storli was your way through to her.

STENSGARD. Well... you know as well as I that if you marry into an uneducated family you end up stuck with the whole bunch of them.

FJELDBO. You said that Monsen was an able man.

STENSGARD. Come on! I know what you think of him.

FJELDBO. He is not blessed with social grace.

STENSGARD. Damn right he isn't! His meetings are more concerned with sausages and beer and the whole house stinks of cheap tobacco.

FJELDBO. It did not appear to concern you before.

STENSGARD. And I had not been here before. I had nothing to compare it with. And I know now how naive I was, I admit it. Allowing myself to be swayed by his people and their ideas, their thirst for power so that they can take over the running of this community for their own purposes. Well, my friend, I am not going to stand up there and use my talents simply to become a spokesman for their selfishness and their vulgarity. They are not true radicals, like me. They have their own self-interest at heart, and nothing else.

FJELDBO. So, tell me, what is the point of the League of Youth?

STENSGARD. To stand up for what is right and to stand firmly against what is wrong.

FJELDBO. And does everyone who has joined your crusade agree with which is which?

STENSGARD. I am a leader, Fjeldbo. It is my job to make the decisions. Just because an idea or a movement has mass support, it does not mean that those who support it understand how best to proceed.

FJELDBO. You are losing me, Stensgard.

STENSGARD. The League cannot be dominated by a narrow base, but reach out, be all-encompassing. Only then can it reach its goal.

FJELDBO. And what is that?

STENSGARD. It will become apparent, we cannot rush these things. But it is imperative that I find a way to best use my abilities.

FJELDBO. Come on, Stensgard, be honest. What is your goal?

STENSGARD. I think I've made myself perfectly clear.

FJELDBO. And now you see that it is the Chamberlain and his connections that will be of more use to you than Monsen.

STENSGARD. That is a ridiculous accusation. I will succeed through my own efforts. And if that requires that I spend more time here, amongst these people, then what of it?

FJELDBO. Here?

STENSGARD. Yes, here. There is a... quality that I can relate to, Fjeldbo. It is not about money or privilege but about something else. Education, knowledge, manners. And what is wrong with admitting that this is something that appeals to me? As long as it does not influence my opinions it can only be of help. It is like drinking a glass of clear cold water. It helps me to think. When I picture Monsen's wealth all I can see are large wads of greasy banknotes and beer-stained mortgage deeds being handed over by fat fingers. How can I strive for something that is noble in that environment?

FJELDBO. I am glad for your sake that Ragna is unable to hear you paint such a flattering picture of her home and family.

STENSGARD. Maybe there is someone else who I am destined to fall in love with.

FJELDBO. I cannot imagine you falling in love with anyone.

STENSGARD *stops for a moment, as though an idea has just come to him.*

STENSGARD. But she is gentle and loyal and elegant. Why wouldn't a man fall in love with such a woman?

FJELDBO. Who?

STENSGARD. Miss Bratsberg of course.

FJELDBO. But yesterday you were devoted to Ragna.

STENSGARD. Who can truly understand the workings of the heart?

FJELDBO. No, Stensgard. I will not stand for it.

STENSGARD. Why not? Do you intend to propose to her?

FJELDBO. I will not have these people being used for your benefit.

STENSGARD. And you see yourself as a defender of the family, do you?

FJELDBO. I see myself as a friend.

STENSGARD. Nonsense. It satisfies your petty vanity to monopolise this house and that is why you want to keep me away.

FJELDBO. I think that would be better for everyone. Yourself included.

STENSGARD. Oh, so now you threaten me.

FJELDBO. You do not understand how things work here.

STENSGARD. Look around you, Fjeldbo, look around and see the influence I have in this town, even though I am as a stranger here to most. See how I am appreciated whilst you continue to be content with your mediocrity.

FJELDBO. You forget that I was welcome in this house a long time before you arrived.

STENSGARD. And now the Chamberlain too appreciates me. Whilst you refuse to.

FJELDBO. What is there to appreciate?

STENSGARD. My will, if nothing else.

ASLAKSEN *enters from the garden*.

ASLAKSEN. Can I finally…

STENSGARD. Yes!

FJELDBO. Come to speak to the great General, have you? Find out what instructions you are to receive as he decides how the world should be run? Well, good luck to you. Good luck to you all!

FJELDBO *exits into the garden*.

STENSGARD. What do you want?

ASLAKSEN. Have you finished the piece?

STENSGARD. What piece?

ASLAKSEN. About the aims of the League.

STENSGARD. I have had other things to deal with.

ASLAKSEN. You said that it was important that you wrote an article to accompany my report.

STENSGARD. Well, I haven't.

ASLAKSEN. Everyone agreed that this would be the best way to proceed.

STENSGARD. It was I who set up the League and I who will decide what is most effective.

ASLAKSEN. Then I will print the report of your speech without your accompanying article.

STENSGARD. And that must be changed.

ASLAKSEN. What?

STENSGARD. You must change your report of the speech.

ASLAKSEN. Why?

STENSGARD. There have been some... developments. As a result of the work I have been undertaking since the League's formation.

ASLAKSEN. I do not understand.

STENSGARD. And as a result what I said about Chamberlain Bratsberg must be edited before you can use it.

ASLAKSEN. How much of it?

STENSGARD. All of it.

ASLAKSEN. But it's been set and is ready to print. I've been working furiously to make sure it's ready.

STENSGARD. Then you have wasted your time.

ASLAKSEN. Everybody is waiting for its publication. There has not been such excitement for years. The elections here are normally of no interest whatsoever but for the first time there is a sense of something new happening. People are expecting to read about what you said and the formation of the League tomorrow morning. This is just what I need for my circulation.

STENSGARD. Oh, so that's what it's all about is it? Your circulation?

ASLAKSEN. No it is not that. You know that I support you and that my paper is at your service. But my paper must also be profitable.

STENSGARD. And my job is to make sure that the League's aims are met by taking the necessary course of action. Not increasing your circulation.

ASLAKSEN. I have nothing to put in its place.

STENSGARD. Listen, Aslaksen, if you do not do as I say and get rid of the report then it will be clear to me that you have decided to exploit the League for your own self-interest.

ASLAKSEN. No, this is not what I am...

STENSGARD. And at that point I will have no choice but to start a rival paper, one that has the best interests of the League at heart. And then where would you be?

ASLAKSEN. You wouldn't do that.

STENSGARD. I would.

ASLAKSEN. I wish you could stand in my place for one day. Stand in my home, with my bed-ridden wife and crippled child.

STENSGARD. Why should I care about worn-out wives and misshapen brats! If you stand in my way, if you dare to provoke me, if you think that you can threaten me, then I promise you that you will be destroyed.

ASLAKSEN. Then I will wait until you think the time is right to print.

STENSGARD. Good. I am glad we could act like men and reach a compromise. The League must come first, Aslaksen. Surely you understand that. We are only the messengers of progress and must not overestimate our own importance.

ASLAKSEN *goes to exit into the garden before remembering his coat and leaving again, passing* LUNDESTAD *who now enters.*

LUNDESTAD. So Aslaksen's rag finally has something of interest to print.

STENSGARD. You seem to have added to the atmosphere with your unexpected announcement.

LUNDESTAD. I am getting old.

STENSGARD. There are many older.

LUNDESTAD. But nonetheless I have been sitting in Parliament for some time now. Maybe it is time for a change. What with all these new ideas that are springing up, ideas that need more nimble minds to fully understand them.

STENSGARD. I'm sure your mind is very nimble.

LUNDESTAD. But I have sided with those of privilege for too long. I do not think a conversion on my part would be very believable.

STENSGARD. And so you are willing to make way for Monsen?

LUNDESTAD. Monsen? No, I would not make way for Monsen. And anyway, even if he does get through the local election he would not have enough support to go on to be selected to sit in Parliament.

STENSGARD. And you're sure of that?

LUNDESTAD. He may win the votes of a certain class of our community...

STENSGARD. It is a developing and strident class...

LUNDESTAD. But to be chosen to sit in Parliament he would have to be selected by his peers, by those in this part of our country who have been victorious in the local elections and who then decide who shall represent them in the Parliament itself. And the old families of property, I promise you, hold sway. They would not want anything to do with a man like Monsen who has hacked down a great deal to make way for himself. Trees and families alike.

STENSGARD. Then why stand down? It makes no sense.

LUNDESTAD. You cannot see it, can you? And I thought that you were an ambitious man.

STENSGARD *is still confused.*

Why do you waste your talents on men like Monsen? What have they really got to offer? Why don't you take this chance to launch your own career? Not just as a leader of this League you have established, but as a real politician.

STENSGARD. Me? But that is not possible. The local election is in two days time and I have had no thought of standing. One day, perhaps, when my talents have been more clearly exhibited. But now is not the time.

LUNDESTAD. The local elections are just a stepping stone; everyone knows that. And are you so sure that there will be a better time? Who knows who will end up in Parliament in my place, and how long they will remain there. It's not a job that many give up lightly. Most would be happy to stay there even after death. And I think a few have probably managed it.

STENSGARD. What are you saying, Mr Lundestad?

LUNDESTAD. Nothing. I apologise. It is wrong of me to try and persuade you to take such action when it is obvious that you do not want to.

LUNDESTAD *goes to leave.*

STENSGARD. No wait! Please. I am ambitious. And the idea of actually having power, real power, of course I often dream of such a thing. But do you really think it is possible? Now?

LUNDESTAD. I do. I would be willing to speak to certain people, to support your candidacy in the local election. It appears to me for a reason I cannot quite fathom that the Chamberlain is very much on your side. And then of course you have your League and there are some of those in it who are eligible to vote.

STENSGARD. Mr Lundestad, I cannot thank you enough.

LUNDESTAD. No, Mr Stensgard, it is I that must thank you. I
have had enough and need to find someone to relieve me of
my burden. If you would accept the challenge then it is you
that is doing me the greatest favour.

STENSGARD. I will not let you down.

LUNDESTAD. So we are agreed.

STENSGARD. Here is my hand.

LUNDESTAD. Excellent! I know that you will not regret this.
But we must proceed carefully.

STENSGARD. What do you suggest?

LUNDESTAD. Collaboration at this stage is essential. We must
make sure that the two victors from the local election are you
and I. Once we have managed that and we have both taken
our place at the regional assembly, I will begin to suggest
you as my successor to Parliament. Subtly of course. And I
will not stand down immediately, that would not play in your
favour at all. No, I will question you a little; give you space
and time to set out your opinions. And then when the time is
right the handover can occur.

STENSGARD. That seems to make sense. I know that you are
greatly respected within the assembly.

LUNDESTAD. All you will need to do is to continue to display
your obvious gifts. And review some of your positions.

STENSGARD. And would that include my championing of the
League of Youth?

LUNDESTAD. Mr Stensgard, I have discovered a simple rule
about politics. There are always fundamentally two parties.
One represents those families who have property,
independence and power. And that is the party I have come to
belong to. Then there is the other party. Made up of those who
desire property, independence and power. Which is the party
that you currently represent. But you will quite naturally leave
this party once you yourself actually acquire power. Not to

mention property and a certain amount of wealth; which is of course essential if you are to take my place in Parliament.

STENSGARD. Yes, I see.

LUNDESTAD. If only you had some prospects.

STENSGARD. Prospects?

LUNDESTAD. A good marriage to a rich heiress. That's all that's needed. And it shouldn't be too difficult. A man like you who could go all the way to the top. Surely no one would be able to turn you down if you played your cards right.

STENSGARD. Of course! Yes! And I do have prospects even if she does not know it yet. And whatever I have to do to get into power, Mr Lundestad, believe me when I say that I will do it honourably.

LUNDESTAD. Then I see certain victory for you. And I shall never forget that you were ready to take the burden of power away from these old shoulders.

And now GUESTS *and* SERVANTS *enter from the garden along with* BRATSBERG, SELMA *and* ERIK, THORA *and* FJELDBO, *and* HEIRE. *As the scene continues* MAIDS *serve refreshments and light lamps as it is now beginning to get darker.*

SELMA. Mr Stensgard, will you join us in a game of forfeits?

STENSGARD. With pleasure. I am in the perfect mood for games.

SELMA *and* STENSGARD *begin to set up chairs and discuss the rules of the game with* THORA *and* ERIK *and some of the other* GUESTS, *as* HEIRE *watches on.*

BRATSBERG *comes up to* LUNDESTAD.

BRATSBERG. I have been looking for you, my dear Lundestad. Is there anything the matter? Why this strange decision of yours?

LUNDESTAD. If a man is being pushed aside by those he has supported, he needs to concentrate on supporting himself.

BRATSBERG. I haven't the faintest idea of what you mean.

LUNDESTAD. I have decided to help to usher in the man you have earmarked as my successor and maintain some dignity in the process.

BRATSBERG. Which man? What on earth is going on?

LUNDESTAD. Stensgard. I suppose that it makes sense for you to try and disarm the more radical element of the district by bringing him under your wing.

BRATSBERG. Well, I am willing to support him in his attacks on the corrupting influence that is emanating from Storli.

LUNDESTAD. And when did you hear these attacks?

BRATSBERG. Last night of course.

LUNDESTAD. Last night?

BRATSBERG. Yes! What's wrong with you, man! When he stood up on that table and started ranting. About greed and the like. Very amusing.

LUNDESTAD. You were amused?

BRATSBERG. I know it is bad manners to revel in such things, but Monsen and his followers got what they deserved. And so we have a duty to support him.

LUNDESTAD. Because of his rant?

BRATSBERG. They will be out for his blood.

LUNDESTAD. On the table?

BRATSBERG. On the table.

LUNDESTAD. About Monsen?

BRATSBERG. I have told everyone what happened. I've been chuckling to myself all day just thinking of it.

LUNDESTAD. And no one has said anything?

BRATSBERG. About what?

THORA. Come on, Father; you must take part in the game.

BRATSBERG. If you say so.

> BRATSBERG *goes over to join* THORA *and the others as the game is beginning.* ERIK, THORA, SELMA *and* STENSGARD *are now sitting down.*

ERIK. Mr Heire, you have been appointed the forfeits judge!

HEIRE. And what a pleasure it would be to judge you all. (*Going over to* LUNDESTAD.) Are you playing too, Mr Lundestad, or just keeping an eye on our conquering hero? He seems to have become quite a favourite around here.

LUNDESTAD. The Chamberlain thinks that the speech that Stensgard made yesterday was attacking Monsen.

HEIRE. Are you sure?

LUNDESTAD. Absolutely. But keep it to yourself. Things are in enough turmoil as it is. And I've been caught up in it more than any other.

THORA. Your Honour, what shall the owner of this forfeit do?

HEIRE. Who has it?

ERIK. Mr Stensgard!

HEIRE. Then please come here, Mr Stensgard.

> STENSGARD *comes over.*

LUNDESTAD. Christ, I've had it up to here with that man.

> LUNDESTAD *exits.*

HEIRE. Now what can you do that will provide us all with even more entertainment than we have been having so far? Oh, I know; you must give a speech.

STENSGARD. About what?

HEIRE. Let us leave that to you, the expert! (*The next part of this is said conspiratorially to* STENSGARD.) This is your chance to make a public apology to the Chamberlain. Do it well and everyone here will see how noble you can be.

STENSGARD. Of course. Thank you.

HEIRE. It is nothing.

BRATSBERG. We are all looking forward to your oratorical skills, Mr Stensgard. But maybe a change in tone from yesterday's broadside?

SELMA. Perhaps you can tell us a fable, Mr Stensgard. With woods and trolls and everything.

BRATSBERG. Perfect. My drink please. Let us all enjoy the talents of our new friend. Come on everyone! Listen to this!

Some more GUESTS *enter from the garden with* FJELDBO *amongst them.*

Ah, Fjeldbo, come and sit next to me. It's time you learnt something of the art of speaking instead of your endless mumbling.

FJELDBO. Of course.

THORA. You may begin, Mr Stensgard.

HEIRE. And do not restrain yourself! We want to see you soar!

STENSGARD. There is a woodcutter, a young woodcutter, brave and handsome, who dreams of finding the perfect tree to chop down so that he can build a boat with which to sail across the oceans.

BRATSBERG. You see, Fjeldbo; he's already got us interested.

STENSGARD. And one day this young man finds himself in a wood that he has never been in before, a wood with all sorts of trees. There are pine trees, and spruce trees, and...

ERIK. He doesn't know any more trees!

BRATSBERG. Ssshh!

STENSGARD. And in the distance he sees smoke and he heads for that smoke and comes to a log cabin with a man sat outside counting his money.

BRATSBERG. And we all know who that's supposed to be. Remember, Mr Stensgard, no more attacks on our Storli friends! Although maybe one more won't harm!

STENSGARD. The money-counter asks our young hero what has brought him to these woods, and the woodcutter tells him of his desire to find a tree to chop down so that he can build a magnificent boat. 'Oh,' the man says, still counting his money, 'I know just the tree that you need. It is the oldest tree in the forest, a tree whose roots go deep down into the ground.'

BRATSBERG (*to* THORA). And that, I suppose, is somehow connected to me.

STENSGARD. 'But let me sharpen your axe for you first,' the money-counter continues, 'as you will need a blade stronger than any other to hack through the bark of this old thing.' And with the axe now gleaming in the sunlight, the woodcutter sets out and soon comes face to face with this ancient tree, in the very heart of the woods. He is just about to raise his axe when a tree troll appears...

SELMA. Thank you, Mr Stensgard...

STENSGARD. ...who tells the woodcutter that this tree is his home, that it is he that looks after these woods, and that nothing can be done here without his permission.

HEIRE. The troll, Mr Stensgard! Tell us more about the troll!

STENSGARD. He is a great troll...

HEIRE. Go on! I want to picture him!

STENSGARD. ...with small beady eyes and a large lumpy nose and bits and pieces of last week's meal stuck to his stringy hair and long matted beard.

BRATSBERG. I do not see why we need trolls in this story at all.

STENSGARD. And the woodcutter says to the troll, 'I am going to chop this old and gnarled tree down. For its roots do nothing but stop the young saplings growing.'

THORA *now looks across at her father rather anxiously, as well as looking at* FJELDBO.

But the troll took hold of the woodcutter and threw him up onto the top branches of this magnificent old tree and said, 'Look at what you see. Look at what grows in the shade that I provide. See the animals that live within me and around me. And see over there the man who counts his money in his cabin and ask yourself "What good he can do for this wood?"'

BRATSBERG. What exactly is this parable about?

THORA. It's just a game, Father.

STENSGARD. And the woodcutter climbed down and looked again at this troll, who no longer appeared gnarled and ugly, but wise and beneficent. And the woodcutter gently laid his axe on the ground.

Chamberlain, I apologise. I was wrong, deeply wrong. I was wrong in wanting to raise my axe to chop you down. I was wrong in seeing you as the one that was strangling new life here in this community. I was wrong to stand on that table and demand that we put an end to the corrupt and suffocating blanket of privilege that I claimed you represented.

THORA. Perhaps we should move on, Mr Stensgard. I think your forfeit has been fulfilled.

STENSGARD. No more will I describe you as a hindrance to progress, as a man who is ignorant of the trends of thought that surround him, as a deadweight pressed down upon the bodies of the young. A toast, my friends! A toast! To Chamberlain Bratsberg! The finest troll in the woods!

There is absolute silence. HEIRE *raises his glass.*

HEIRE. I believe a toast has been offered.

One by one the GUESTS *raise their glasses. There is a sense of total disbelief and embarrassment.*

GUESTS. To Chamberlain Bratsberg!

BRATSBERG. Well, thank you, Mr Stensgard, but please do excuse me.

THORA *and* FJELDBO *go up to* BRATSBERG *to exit with him.* BRATSBERG *snaps at* FJELDBO.

Leave me alone, you fool!

STENSGARD *is oblivious to what has happened.*

STENSGARD. Right, shall we continue with the game? I think that went rather well, don't you?

Lights.

End of Act One.

ACT TWO

The next morning. BRATSBERG*'s office. There is a portrait of his father on the wall. A large and ornate desk. A door leads off to the drawing room.* THORA *and* SELMA *are sat on a sofa with* FJELDBO *standing next to them.* BRATSBERG *is pacing up and down.*

BRATSBERG. The absolute indignity of it!

THORA. Calm down, Father.

SELMA. It was a story, surely…

BRATSBERG. To have that windbag in my house – my house! – describe me in such a way.

FJELDBO. I am sorry that he ever came to our town.

BRATSBERG. And you can be quiet. Telling me that he was talking about Monsen during his preposterous outburst. That's what started the whole sorry situation in the first place.

THORA. He was only trying to help, Father.

BRATSBERG. He is incapable of helping.

THORA. That is not fair. He has always been here when we need him.

FJELDBO. I merely wanted to save you embarrassment.

BRATSBERG. And is that what has been achieved? Well, has it? No! No, it hasn't. I have had to sit there amongst my guests whilst I have been ridiculed.

SELMA. But, Chamberlain, everyone knows that…

BRATSBERG. First these vulgar Storli people moan about my influence, then Lundestad foolishly declares he is to give up his seat in Parliament, and now I have this upstart worming his way into my affections and my household because of you.

THORA. Father!

BRATSBERG. And what will they all be saying? I'll tell you. That I have been hoodwinked into joining forces with this idiot radical because I am intimidated by him.

THORA. Then perhaps you should have taken more notice in the first place. He has been making endless pronouncements ever since he arrived.

BRATSBERG. That is not my job. I do not bother myself with speeches or local politics or these silly Leagues of Youth. Once you delve into that world then you are already doomed to drown in muck. I have to stand aloof from that nonsense. And people should understand that; like they used to.

SELMA. Perhaps there is something in what he is saying?

THORA *looks at* SELMA, *indicating that she should shut up.*

BRATSBERG. With the greatest respect, my dear Selma, you have absolutely no understanding at all of these matters.

THORA. Things are changing.

BRATSBERG. Yes! There used to be respect. Now what do we get? This whole community is beginning to collapse around my ears. And it is Monsen and his kind that are to blame.

There is a knock on the door.

Come in!

STENSGARD *enters.*

You!

STENSGARD. Good morning, Chamberlain; ladies. I have been made aware by my good friend here…

FJELDBO *raises his hand to protest his innocence.*

…that I may have inadvertently caused you some discomfort.

BRATSBERG. Really? And I suppose you are now going to explain how it's all down to some terrible misunderstanding.

STENSGARD. No, I am here because I am in love with your daughter. And I have come to ask for her hand.

FJELDBO. Are you insane, man?

STENSGARD. You have only seen me twice, Chamberlain, and I am painfully aware that on both occasions I have not appeared to you in the most favourable light. In time you will get to know me better.

BRATSBERG. I think I have seen enough. I think we have all seen enough. You are not welcome here.

STENSGARD. But it is this beautiful home of yours, these charming people, that have made me understand that this is the environment I need to become the person that I must.

THORA. Mr Stensgard, my father has asked you to leave.

STENSGARD. You are a dutiful daughter and I understand that you must set your heart against me to please your father.

BRATSBERG. Did you not hear what I said?

STENSGARD. Chamberlain! I know that it is I that am seeking your acceptance, but you must also be aware of the benefits such an alliance would bring to you. Your family is loved in this town; it has stood proudly at the pinnacle of this community through generations. And I respect that deeply. But it has to have new blood injected into it. Otherwise it will simply... deteriorate.

BRATSBERG. This is unconscionable!

STENSGARD. I understand your inability to see things in any other way than through the eyes of tradition and custom. But this is not what the world is to become. Surely it is character that really counts, not ancestry; character and judgement. And once you both get to know me then you will grow fond of me. Like everyone else.

BRATSBERG. What do you think of this, doctor?

FJELDBO. I think he is mad.

STENSGARD. I may appear forthright, but would you rather I was a docile man, like Fjeldbo here? Someone unable to rise to a challenge for fear of upsetting anyone? I have a mission to fulfil and blind prejudice must not halt that. You have iron in your works, Chamberlain, and I have iron in my soul!

BRATSBERG. Get out!

STENSGARD. But I do not understand.

BRATSBERG. And never return again.

STENSGARD. I am trying to make amends.

BRATSBERG. And you have failed.

STENSGARD. Can you not appreciate the honesty and integrity of my character in being so open with you?

SELMA. Mr Stensgard, I think that you should listen to…

STENSGARD. Look at the League. How men have come flocking. Think what I may go on to achieve.

BRATSBERG. All men like you can achieve is to wreck what has taken generations to build.

STENSGARD. I ask you one more time to reconsider.

BRATSBERG. Then you are a fool greater than any I have ever seen in my life.

STENSGARD. I take that as a rejection then.

FJELDBO. I think it is.

STENSGARD. Without any consideration of the consequences?

BRATSBERG. And what do you suppose a man like you can really do to a man like me?

STENSGARD. You cannot see it, can you? You cannot see how I am gathering the forces of change around me, like a storm. How I have the power to decide whether or not to crush you. And to leave you crawling from this town a broken man, with all of your precious heritage crashing around your ears.

BRATSBERG. Fjeldbo is right. You are insane.

STENSGARD. No, Chamberlain, I am driven. It is not my choice, but my duty, as someone charged with ushering in the new. Please sleep on what I have said. You may not be able to see my worth but I think that even though she dare not admit it, your daughter does. That is all I ask, Chamberlain, that your prejudice against me does not prevent her from leading a happy and fulfilling life. Ladies.

STENSGARD *exits.*

BRATSBERG. Unbelievable. I apologise for what you have just encountered; you must both put it out of your minds immediately. And why did you not stand up for yourself?

FJELDBO. I was more concerned with the attack on you than on me.

BRATSBERG. Oh, nonsense. Stensgard is right. You are docile. Always creeping around like a cat that is trying to find somewhere better to sleep. How exactly have you managed to become such a frequent visitor here?

THORA. Please let us not argue amongst ourselves.

FJELDBO. Absolutely. It is Stensgard that we must watch out for.

BRATSBERG. There you go again, agreeing with everything.

FJELDBO. I am sorry, but you must know that I will stand up for you. I will do whatever you request of me… I would willingly…

BRATSBERG *holds up his hand towards* FJELDBO, *who immediately stops what he is saying. He looks briefly at* THORA *and then stands there silently, with an air of embarrassment lingering over him.*

BRATSBERG. Maybe it is better to have an insane belief in your own abilities than to merely slink about in the shadows.

SELMA. Perhaps we have all forgotten what happens when people are passionate.

BRATSBERG. Please leave me. All of you.

THORA, FJELDBO and SELMA exit. BRATSBERG is left alone for a moment. He is at a loss to understand what is happening to his world. THORA enters again.

THORA. There is someone else to see you, Father. He has been waiting by the back door.

BRATSBERG. Well, send them in. It cannot be as much a surprise as my last guest.

THORA exits, and a moment later MONSEN enters.

MONSEN. Chamberlain.

BRATSBERG. Mr Monsen. What is it I can do for you?

MONSEN. Can we talk, man to man?

BRATSBERG. We can.

MONSEN. You do not look kindly at my business.

BRATSBERG. I don't believe your business is affected by how I look at it.

MONSEN. Probably not. But even you will agree that I have worked hard.

BRATSBERG. There is nothing wrong with working hard.

MONSEN. And now I think it is time to scale down my operations.

BRATSBERG. You hope to take Lundestad's seat in Parliament perhaps?

MONSEN. I'm afraid that Stensgard has rather pissed in my pot, if you'll excuse the expression, Chamberlain. I've left the field open to him.

BRATSBERG. Well, I'm sure if he does come to anything you'll be able to find a use for him.

MONSEN. Like you and Lundestad?

BRATSBERG. He can look after himself.

MONSEN. I'm sure he can. Anyway, I do not think I was made for that kind of life. I have had a good run, a very good run...

BRATSBERG. Congratulations.

MONSEN....and there is no point in working myself into the grave. A man should enjoy his money, as I'm sure you agree. So I am here to offer you a favour. When the woods at Langerud were auctioned off five years ago you were bidding...

BRATSBERG. And you outbid me.

MONSEN. And now you can have them. The sawmills too.

BRATSBERG. After that unholy hacking down which you have carried out?

MONSEN. They are still worth a lot, and with your experience then in a few years time you will...

BRATSBERG. Thank you but it is not a matter I wish to get involved in.

MONSEN. I will be frank with you. I have plans for a large investment and I need capital.

BRATSBERG. I'm sure there are others you can go to.

MONSEN. They are all tied up.

BRATSBERG. I wonder why.

MONSEN. And so you can have the woods for next to nothing.

BRATSBERG. I don't want them at any price.

MONSEN *is taken aback by this and is unsure of how to continue.*

MONSEN. It is a generous offer.

BRATSBERG. Which I decline.

MONSEN. And I can't twist your arm?

BRATSBERG. No.

MONSEN. You surprise me. There's still money in those woods.

BRATSBERG. I have other woods.

MONSEN. You do see that I am trying to build bridges between us?

BRATSBERG. It appears so.

MONSEN. Then I hope you think it's fair enough if I now ask something of you.

BRATSBERG. What do you want?

MONSEN. Just your backing. Your name. As security.

BRATSBERG. You dare come to me with such a request?

MONSEN. I will pay for it. You will get a fair price when the deal goes through.

BRATSBERG. You think my name can simply be bought?

Again MONSEN *is stumped. It is not going as planned.*

MONSEN. What harm have I ever done you? How have I affected your business?

BRATSBERG. It is the way that you go about things.

MONSEN. And that's why I am treated like this? Because of the way that I 'go about things'?

BRATSBERG. No! It is not just that. It is the way that you have changed the tone of this town. The way that things now operate.

MONSEN. What are you on about?

BRATSBERG. I created a savings bank at my works for the benefit of my employees and others. But then you started one too.

MONSEN. Is that a crime?

BRATSBERG. I lost my customers. They went to you.

MONSEN. Because I pay a higher rate of interest on their savings.

BRATSBERG. And charge a higher rate for borrowing.

MONSEN. But I don't insist on the need for endless proof of security like you do.

BRATSBERG. And then what happens? People start believing that they are businessmen and run around making deals when in reality they haven't got a penny to their name.

MONSEN. People have to start somewhere.

BRATSBERG. But it makes no sense. Why can't they just stick to what they know?

MONSEN. Like I should have?

BRATSBERG. What was wrong with being a lumberman? Was it the fact that you were in my service that offended you? Your father did not mind. He earned his living honestly and was a well-regarded man.

MONSEN. Who worked himself like a donkey and ended up going down the falls in his raft. You have no idea, do you? Of the lives of those that slave away for you in your forests, whilst you sit sipping brandy in front of the fire and the money simply piles up. How can you blame anyone for wanting to work their way out of it?

BRATSBERG. But by what means have you risen? First by selling schnapps; then buying up bad debts and recovering them mercilessly, until you had enough capital to move forward. How many people have you ruined, so that you could improve yourself?

MONSEN. That is the way that business works. One man's gain is another man's loss. As Daniel Heire will tell you.

BRATSBERG. When this country was in need, after the secession from Denmark, my late father helped out beyond his means and parts of our estate were sold to the Heire family. And look what happened. Daniel had the woods cut down to the detriment of all who lived on the estate. He did not know what he was doing and it was my duty to prevent it continuing. I had the law on my side. I was in the right when I claimed back my property.

MONSEN. I have not gone against the law either.

BRATSBERG. But can you not see what is happening? People no longer ask how a fortune was acquired or how long it has been in the family; they only ask how much it is worth. And now you and I are lumped together because we are the biggest owners of properties here. And I cannot tolerate it!

MONSEN. I am asking for your assistance.

BRATSBERG. And I cannot help you.

MONSEN. Even though you know that your own son stands to make a large amount of money from this deal.

BRATSBERG. Erik?

MONSEN. Yes. He did tell you what it was for, didn't he?

BRATSBERG. What are you on about?

MONSEN. When you agreed to sign as guarantor for his bill?

BRATSBERG. What bill?

MONSEN. The bill for ten thousand dollars.

BRATSBERG. I do not understand.

MONSEN. There was only so much I could lend him and so he presented a bill at my bank that you had guaranteed. And then used that money, with the rest, to come in on this investment.

BRATSBERG. I have never acted as a guarantor for anyone, nor will I.

MONSEN. In which case your son must have been more desperate than I thought.

BRATSBERG. You are making no sense.

MONSEN. Your signature must have been forged.

BRATSBERG. Get out! Get out! You have brought nothing but avarice and corruption to our community. I see your fine guests travel along the country roads like a pack of howling wolves! And everyone knows how you treat your maids. And that your wife has lost her mind because of your depravity.

MONSEN. Watch your mouth!

BRATSBERG. Or?

MONSEN. You will regret it. I can bring the great and noble Bratsbergs down with one piece of paper.

BRATSBERG. Damn you, Monsen, and do not think that you can ever threaten me. You asked what I had against you. Well, now you know. Now you know why I have you barred from respectable society. That is the way out!

MONSEN. I know the way, Bratsberg!

MONSEN *exits*.

BRATSBERG. Fjeldbo! Fjeldbo! Come here!

FJELDBO *enters*.

FJELDBO. What is it, Chamberlain?

BRATSBERG. Nobody would listen! Everyone said that I was exaggerating when I could see that Monsen was corrupting the soul of our community.

FJELDBO. What has happened?

BRATSBERG. There is a forged bill with my name on it.

FJELDBO. Who did this?

BRATSBERG. My son is involved in some way.

FJELDBO. But surely you do not think that...

BRATSBERG. I do not know what to think! I have warned him, told him. And now he has done this. But no... no it cannot be. Monsen is simply lying or maybe Erik has been tricked in some way. Signing something not knowing what it was. You know how unworldly he is in the ways of business. Oh, how Monsen must have loved getting his hands on him. A Bratsberg! You understand now why I have to oversee everything? The chaos that would ensue if I were ever to hand over the reins?

ERIK *enters*.

ERIK. My dear father.

BRATSBERG. You. (*To* FJELDBO.) Go. See what you can find out for me, Fjeldbo.

FJELDBO. Of course.

FJELDBO *exits*.

ERIK. I see that Monsen has just left here.

BRATSBERG. Yes.

ERIK. What did he want?

BRATSBERG. He informed me of your business dealings together.

ERIK. I am sorry, Father. I did not think you would approve.

BRATSBERG. I hear he has lent you money.

ERIK. I did not want to ask for money from you.

BRATSBERG. And so what exactly did you do, Erik?

ERIK. What do you mean?

BRATSBERG. To get this money.

ERIK. I have borrowed from him. I am sorry. It was a mistake.

BRATSBERG. How dare you associate our name with that man? Can you not see the damage it may cause? I have a title that has been given to me by the King. People understand that I represent what is best about our town and our country. You have your mother's inheritance. You and Selma have been given a home in which to live.

ERIK. I have to make my own way, Father.

BRATSBERG. But you are a Bratsberg! Think of what you will inherit.

ERIK. But what can I do until then? You run the ironworks yourself and oversee the management of your land and property. You do not trust me with anything. How can I make a life for myself? And when I see these people who have made a fortune out of nothing.

BRATSBERG. But how is that possible? How? It cannot be done without getting one's hands dirty. And the same goes for one's conscience.

The two men look at each other, both waiting for the next move.

ERIK. Father, I need to borrow some money.

BRATSBERG. Oh no. I will not do that. I will not have you coming here, begging me...

ERIK. Please, Father... I am sorry... just this once... I swear that I will never come to you again. But the interest on the loan is due and Monsen is demanding I repay it. He needs money, you see.

BRATSBERG. I know. And if you cannot pay?

ERIK. Then I stand to lose everything I have. More than I have.

BRATSBERG. It will be an expensive lesson.

ERIK. But my honour; my name; our name!

BRATSBERG. You think that honour is to be gained by becoming a successful businessman?

ERIK. You do not understand.

BRATSBERG. Oh, I understand! I understand that maybe I should just let Mr Stensgard and his League of Youth sweep everything of value away in the elections tomorrow. That maybe he is right and his time has come after all.

BRATSBERG *goes back to his work, ignoring* ERIK. ERIK *stands there for a moment, unsure of what to do next, before leaving quietly.* BRATSBERG *sits down and pours himself a drink. He shakes his head, utterly defeated as the lights fade. As this happens we see a* CROWD *of people entering the theatre from the auditorium. It is the following day, election day, and there is much conversation and a sense of election-fever.*

A large banner with 'The League of Youth' written on it is unfurled in the auditorium, as ASLAKSEN *arrives with a pile of newspapers which he hands out to the* CROWD. *This pile is now diminished as he has been doing this since the early morning and it is now mid-afternoon.*

The scene behind this action changes so that we are now in a room at MADAM RUNDHOLM'*s inn which is being used as the hustings. The actual voting area is just offstage through a door. To the side of this door there is a desk with ink, paper and a pen. We will see* MEN *coming and going to vote throughout the scene, into this offstage area, which should feel like a place of debate and excitement.*

STENSGARD *enters with* BASTIAN, *strides up to* ASLAKSEN *and eagerly gets hold of a paper which he begins to read.*

STENSGARD. There you are; I've been looking for you all day. Where is it?

ASLAKSEN. Here. 'Independence Day Celebrations from our Special Correspondent.' That's me. I put all of the offensive words in bold.

STENSGARD. It looks like all of it's in bold.

ASLAKSEN. Well, it is mostly.

STENSGARD. Have they been distributed?

ASLAKSEN. Yes.

STENSGARD. And have the League's supporters roused themselves?

BASTIAN. They have all been coming. Even the ones who cannot vote.

STENSGARD. I'm not bothered about them. (*To* BASTIAN.) You must go and talk to those voters who haven't made their minds up yet. Tell Lundestad's supporters that he and I agree on everything. And Monsen's that we stand shoulder to shoulder on policy.

BASTIAN. And who is the Chamberlain supporting?

ASLAKSEN. No one knows. All these pacts and coalitions have caused huge excitement and utter bewilderment. There are whole swathes of people who have no idea who they're really voting for. But they've been in there since Madam Rundholm opened her doors.

STENSGARD. Go.

BASTIAN *exits into the voting area.*

It would be helpful to know what the Chamberlain is saying.

ASLAKSEN. You must hope that you have done enough. He will never suggest that anyone vote for you or Lundestad now that the old farmer has turned against him. He will do everything he can to block your way.

STENSGARD. Let me show you something.

STENSGARD *pulls an envelope from his pocket and takes out a bill from it.*

ASLAKSEN. What is it?

STENSGARD. A bill made out to Erik Bratsberg that has been guaranteed by the Chamberlain.

ASLAKSEN. Why do you have this?

STENSGARD. Monsen gave it to me. He came round last night and said that if I felt the need that I should use it. That it may not be all that it seems.

ASLAKSEN. Is he suggesting that it is forged?

STENSGARD. I don't know.

ASLAKSEN. But if it is, why give it to you? Surely he could use something like this himself.

STENSGARD. Perhaps he thinks it will help buy him influence.

ASLAKSEN. And are you going to use it? If so, you should let the Chamberlain know that you have it immediately, to keep him quiet.

STENSGARD. A man must win the support of the people through the power of his arguments alone.

ASLAKSEN. But it might be the diff...

STENSGARD. Through argument and through organisation. Not blackmail. How can one hope to change things fundamentally if power is not won honestly and openly?

ASLAKSEN. You are right. I should never have suggested...

STENSGARD. Although when you are up against the full force of the establishment, with all of its resources ready to assemble against you; and when the gains are so great, and it is the masses that will ultimately benefit, then the use of this as a way of silencing Bratsberg could quite clearly be seen as morally admissible.

ASLAKSEN. So are you going to use it or aren't you? If so, you must move quickly. There will not be many left to come now but their votes could be crucial.

STENSGARD. If only I wasn't so alone in all of this. Go on, do what I say and rally the vote. And please, Aslaksen, don't drink!

ASLAKSEN *exits into the voting area, and* MADAM RUNDHOLM *enters. She has dressed up for the occasion.*

MADAM RUNDHOLM. I have never known my establishment to be so busy, Mr Stensgard. These elections are normally the most dreary affairs. I'm not sure that I have enough champagne in.

STENSGARD. Make sure you keep a bottle for later.

MADAM RUNDHOLM. I wouldn't be too confident. The Chamberlain usually manages to get his way.

STENSGARD. Maybe not this time.

MADAM RUNDHOLM. I hear there is a little plan for you to go on to take a seat in Parliament, if you get elected.

STENSGARD. Do you?

MADAM RUNDHOLM. Not much is kept secret in a place like this.

STENSGARD. Well, if that were to pass then be sure that I will stand up for your concerns, Madam Rundholm.

MADAM RUNDHOLM. It's a shame that I cannot vote then, isn't it?

HEIRE *enters*.

HEIRE. Good afternoon. I hope I am not interrupting.

MADAM RUNDHOLM. Of course not.

HEIRE. Look how she sparkles! What a waste to be unmarried.

MADAM RUNDHOLM. I sometimes think so too.

HEIRE. Especially as the blissful state of matrimony has already been experienced. The late Rundholm was a magnificent example.

MADAM RUNDHOLM. He was a useless drunk. But a husband is a husband.

HEIRE. And a widow is a widow.

MADAM RUNDHOLM. And business is business. And I need to get more champagne. So please excuse me.

MADAM RUNDHOLM *exits*.

HEIRE. A substantial woman, Mr Stensgard. Clever and sprightly, no children to wear her down, and well-read. Although I am sure you have other things on your mind today.

STENSGARD. Yes. It is an exciting moment. Democracy in action, Mr Heire! People rising from their slumber, knowing that their dreams were stirred by the vision of liberty and that today this dream can be made real.

HEIRE. And there was I dreaming of beef. Thank the Lord they have taken my vote away.

FJELDBO *enters*.

And here's the doctor. Obviously in the cause of science.

FJELDBO. Science?

HEIRE. To observe the epidemic which surrounds us. A malignant strain of rabies agitatoria! Good and honest men running around like frightened chickens not knowing which perch to sit on. Excuse me, my young friends. I must partake again of this excitement before it all fades back into nothingness.

HEIRE *exits into the voting area.*

STENSGARD. Have you seen the Chamberlain today?

FJELDBO. Yes.

STENSGARD. What did he say?

FJELDBO. About what?

STENSGARD. About my declaration to Thora.

FJELDBO. Do you really think that he would have considered it? You do, don't you? You are so blind that you actually...

STENSGARD. Well, maybe I will find a way to persuade him to come round to me. You are here to vote?

FJELDBO. I am ineligible, as you know. But I have the Chamberlain's paper.

STENSGARD. On another errand, like a faithful little dog?

FJELDBO. He is not voting for you, of course.

STENSGARD. Then for Lundestad, I presume.

FJELDBO. No. For the district councillor and the dean.

STENSGARD. After all that Lundestad has done for him over the years.

FJELDBO. He knows of the pact you have made, and has told those who respect him not to vote for either of you. You have not won yet.

STENSGARD. If I am elected, I shall attack him with all guns blazing.

FJELDBO. I would not get ahead of yourself. It is a big step from getting through the local election to being chosen to sit in Parliament. Lundestad knows what he is doing by allying himself with you. What makes you think he will stand by what he has said?

STENSGARD. If he doesn't honour our agreement then I will agitate against him. I have my League to assist me.

FJELDBO. But to be eligible to enter Parliament you will need to be more financially secure.

STENSGARD. Of course.

FJELDBO. Which is why you want to marry Miss Bratsberg?

STENSGARD. You would marry her too. I see you lapping around her ankles.

FJELDBO. I know the Chamberlain would not accept me as a son even if she would take my hand. For some reason he has begun to distrust me ever since you arrived.

STENSGARD. Is that why you scorn me?

FJELDBO. I do not understand why you would want to marry into a family when you seek to destroy what they stand for?

STENSGARD. Because I need room to breathe. To think! How can I plan for the good of the people when I have to spend all of my time drinking schnapps with them or laughing at their beery jokes? The Chamberlain stands in the way of progress because he cannot understand it. The privilege that he feels is owed to him sits in his blood without him being aware of it. By welcoming me into his family all of that can change. I can use that wealth and comfort for the benefit of others.

FJELDBO. How?

STENSGARD. By being able to escape from the clutches of the people, I can work unhindered for the benefit of the people.

FJELDBO. Listen to me, man, I am warning you. Keep away from Miss Bratsberg for your own sake.

LUNDESTAD *enters*.

LUNDESTAD. Ah, here we are. Our fate is almost decided then.

STENSGARD. Fjeldbo is about to cast the Chamberlain's vote. Neither you nor I are on that bit of paper.

LUNDESTAD. That is to be expected.

STENSGARD. You did not think he would vote for you one last time? One simple act of generosity for all your years of support?

LUNDESTAD. Well, maybe I needed him as much as he needed me.

STENSGARD. Go on then, Fjeldbo. Do your duty.

FJELDBO. I would not drink to the success of your pact yet, gentlemen.

FJELDBO *exits into the voting area.*

LUNDESTAD. It seems to be going well. For you anyway.

STENSGARD. We need you to be elected too.

LUNDESTAD. It will be close.

STENSGARD *takes the bill from his pocket and gives it to* LUNDESTAD.

What is it?

STENSGARD. Tell me if you think this is forged?

HEIRE *enters again.*

HEIRE. Ah, gentlemen. What a picture! The dying oak offering shade to the young sapling.

STENSGARD. Is Aslaksen in there?

HEIRE. An excellent lieutenant. Rounding up the last dregs of the vote. And a hearty toast for everyone.

STENSGARD. I asked him not to drink.

HEIRE. It's a heightened atmosphere. Especially since these new rumours have been wafted amongst us.

STENSGARD. Is someone else's campaign gathering momentum? Surely not the dean's or the district councillor?

HEIRE. No, this is much more exciting. A great bankruptcy is in our midst. Not politically of course, Mr Lundestad.

STENSGARD. Bankruptcy?

HEIRE. A totally unexpected one, they say.

STENSGARD. But who is it?

HEIRE. Ah, you will excuse me again then, gentlemen, whilst I dig into things a little and find out which of our moneyed friends is to come crashing down.

HEIRE *exits*.

STENSGARD. Do you know anything of this?

LUNDESTAD. You asked if this bill was forged.

STENSGARD. Yes.

LUNDESTAD. That is not the Chamberlain's signature.

STENSGARD. But would his son do such a thing?

LUNDESTAD. I would never have believed it; but who knows what people can be driven to.

STENSGARD. My God! Do you think this could be connected to what Heire just told us?

LUNDESTAD. I wouldn't like to say. But if Erik has done this then it would be because he has gone in too far over his head and needs to get hold of ready cash. And if he couldn't get hold of it then his father would need to help out. And if the Chamberlain's money is tied up then that would mean auctioning properties and...

STENSGARD....it must be so! That is why Bratsberg speaks with such disgust of Monsen. Because he has undermined his own wealth. And now the day of reckoning has come. Oh yes, Lundestad, things are truly beginning to fall apart.

LUNDESTAD. And is such destruction what you really want?

STENSGARD. We must uproot before we can rebuild. And if the Chamberlain is laid low then he will not be able to stand in the way of my marriage to his daughter.

LUNDESTAD. Though, of course, if the family was to be bankrupt you would not have the property qualification to allow you to enter into Parliament. And our agreement would be meaningless.

STENSGARD *suddenly looks very pained.*

Are you all right? Oh, of course. What an old fool I am. Dear Mr Stensgard, if you truly love the girl what difference does it make if she is rich or poor?

STENSGARD. None.

LUNDESTAD. Exactly. A happy marriage is not founded on money. I know that.

STENSGARD. Fjeldbo was trying to warn me to keep away. Like the good friend that deep down he knows that he is.

LUNDESTAD. Your day will come. Do not be scared of hard times. A happy home, a loyal wife. What more could a man want? A place in Parliament is not everything. And one day, when you have built yourself up, you will acquire the property and wealth necessary to try for power again. And you will have more experience then as well. Yes, maybe it is for the best.

STENSGARD. But what will happen to you? I was to take the weight of responsibility from your shoulders. To ease your burden.

LUNDESTAD. Oh well, I will have to soldier on. It is the way of it. I would not dream of asking you to sacrifice love because of me.

STENSGARD. That is very noble of you.

LUNDESTAD. We are noble men.

STENSGARD. And I can be nobler still.

LUNDESTAD. You are noble enough.

STENSGARD. No, I will sacrifice love.

LUNDESTAD. Nonsense, I will not hear of it.

STENSGARD. I must.

LUNDESTAD. You really have no need to. I will be able to struggle on for a bit longer. A year or two; maybe more.

STENSGARD. No! I declare here and now that I decline the happiness of working in poverty for the one I love. Because I belong to the people! Yes, Lundestad, I am their servant; and I will do as they bid me!

LUNDESTAD. Well, Mr Stensgard, you never cease to surprise me.

He shakes his hand and then exits into the voting area.
BASTIAN *comes over to* STENSGARD.

BASTIAN. And now we will see a force flowing through this town greater than any mountain river. And just as the thunderous volumes of water carry all in its path, so too will we!

STENSGARD. What ridiculous overblown rhetoric.

BASTIAN. I am quoting from your article.

STENSGARD. Of course... but context... without context it is... Look, why are you imitating me?

BASTIAN. What do you mean?

STENSGARD. I can see it. How the League's followers are taking me as some kind of model. Look at your clothes.

BASTIAN. I always wear these...

STENSGARD. I want you to stop it, Bastian! I want all of you to stop it! People should think for themselves in our party, not blindly follow the words of one man.

BASTIAN. Of course.

STENSGARD. Make sure you tell them.

BASTIAN. I will do as you say.

STENSGARD. Good.

BASTIAN. And in return, I wonder if you can do me a favour.

STENSGARD. It is a busy time...

BASTIAN. I want to get married.

STENSGARD. Who to?

BASTIAN. Sssshhh! In this house.

STENSGARD. Madam Rundholm?

BASTIAN. Yes. Please put in a good word for me, my friend. Use your eloquence for my benefit. She has a good business here and knows many people. If I marry her then maybe the council work will come too.

STENSGARD. You talk of marriage and road works in the same breath?

BASTIAN. My bridge-building has improved greatly.

STENSGARD. But such a union must be based solely on the foundations of love. This is sordid.

BASTIAN. Please! I have asked Ragna to say something, but...

And now STENSGARD *understands what he needs to do, and grabs* BASTIAN *by the shoulders.*

STENSGARD. Of course I will speak to Madam Rundholm.

BASTIAN. Really? But you just said that it was sordid.

STENSGARD. Nonsense. You misheard. But you must also agree to speak for me.

BASTIAN. What do you mean?

STENSGARD. Surely you must have noticed?

BASTIAN. Noticed what?

STENSGARD. How I too have fallen in love?

BASTIAN. No.

STENSGARD. Do not be so modest. You, the man who can spot every tiny and important detail. The great bridge-builder of our time.

BASTIAN. Well... yes... I... did have an inkling.

STENSGARD. Your sister! Ragna!

BASTIAN. I know! But I heard that you had made an approach to the Chamberlain's daughter.

STENSGARD. I was trying to strengthen the League. To curry favour so that we might progress in our aims, comrade.

BASTIAN. I see.

STENSGARD. Then you will speak to her? This angel who fires my soul?

BASTIAN. Here is my hand on it.

STENSGARD. How blessed we both are to have hearts that beat with such pure feeling.

MADAM RUNDHOLM *enters carrying a crate of champagne, causing* BASTIAN *to exit into the voting area.*

BASTIAN. Speak well for me.

MADAM RUNDHOLM. Still here, Mr Stensgard?

STENSGARD. I do not have a fine house to run my operations from, but I am confident that things seem to be working in my favour.

MADAM RUNDHOLM. There are a lot of very old men being wheeled out. I can't imagine they will be voting for you.

STENSGARD. Listen; may I speak in confidence?

MADAM RUNDHOLM. Of course.

STENSGARD. You and Daniel Heire were talking just now of your... single state.

MADAM RUNDHOLM. He is an old fool.

STENSGARD. But if a suitable man were to turn up?

MADAM RUNDHOLM. It is not easy being a widow.

STENSGARD. Someone who had been pining for you in silence…

MADAM RUNDHOLM. And it is not polite to make fun of me…

STENSGARD. A young man who has prospects, who is ready to build for the future, and who is also lonely…

MADAM RUNDHOLM. Lonely? I cannot imagine that…

STENSGARD. Oh yes. It is so.

MADAM RUNDHOLM. And you are not playing games with me?

STENSGARD. Why do you think I would do that? When you have the power in your hands to shape a person's happiness.

MADAM RUNDHOLM. Then yes, yes of course I would consider it, Mr Stensgard. I would be a fool not to.

RAGNA *enters*.

RAGNA. Is my father here, Madam Rundholm?

MADAM RUNDHOLM. No, Ragna. He has gone to Oslo. He came round first thing this morning to ask for some money.

RAGNA. That is impossible. How could he?

RAGNA *goes to leave*.

MADAM RUNDHOLM. Don't go! There is news to celebrate. Please just wait while I run down to the cellar and fetch a bottle of the good stuff. This is just for the customers.

RAGNA. No, I must…

MADAM RUNDHOLM *exits*.

STENSGARD. Are you all right?

RAGNA. I must go. They will be on their way. Unless they have already met him on the road.

STENSGARD. Who?

RAGNA. I'm sorry, I must get back. Please excuse me.

STENSGARD *blocks her path.*

STENSGARD. Ragna. Why do you ignore me?

RAGNA. Mr Stensgard, I must go.

STENSGARD. No; I won't let you.

RAGNA. Not now; please. You do not understand.

STENSGARD. I understand that it was my good fortune that brought you here at this moment.

RAGNA. I beg of you to let me pass.

STENSGARD. The vote appears to be going well for me.

RAGNA. Then I am pleased for you. Now if I may...

STENSGARD. Why are you like this? You used to enjoy my company.

RAGNA. Can you not see that I am anxious to leave?

STENSGARD. When I came to Storli you were always eager to talk to me.

RAGNA. I am not sure if that was exactly the case.

STENSGARD. Then tell me.

RAGNA. Tell you what?

STENSGARD. Tell me what has turned you against me. What is it that people have been saying that has made you act towards me in this way?

RAGNA. It is you, Mr Stensgard. Nobody has had to say anything. I simply got to know you better; that is all.

STENSGARD. What do you mean?

RAGNA. Please; you must let me go.

STENSGARD. Then of course. I would never wish to detain
you against your wishes.

RAGNA. Thank you.

Blocking her path again.

STENSGARD. But listen to me, Ragna. I know that people
have denigrated me, because of this campaign. I have heard
the whispers. And I have had my attention turned, I know
that. But let us remember how things were when I first
arrived. I know that this is not the best time but I cannot help
myself... I must declare my love for you, Ragna.

RAGNA. Mr Stensgard...

STENSGARD. You know what is happening here in this town.
How my arrival has brought a new energy to this place. And
I have to find a woman who is good enough to join me on
this journey.

RAGNA. I am flattered but...

STENSGARD. You are the one, Ragna. I have chosen you.
Please say that I may come and talk to you about this
further?

RAGNA. Yes, yes, you may. But I really do have to leave now.

STENSGARD. And I look forward to us renewing our
charming conversation.

RAGNA *exits as* MADAM RUNDHOLM *enters with wine
and cakes.*

MADAM RUNDHOLM. Is Ragna not staying?

STENSGARD. No. She has much to think about.

MADAM RUNDHOLM. Well, let us drink a toast. To the
promises that love may offer.

STENSGARD. And for the luck in love that we both deserve.

They drink. HEIRE *enters.*

HEIRE. And still the turmoil continues. It's like watching fish in a net, squirming amongst themselves without any idea of what they're really trying to do.

MADAM RUNDHOLM. And I suppose I should go and see if the vote has concluded.

MADAM RUNDHOLM *exits*.

HEIRE. She seems to be very fond of you. You should get your teeth stuck in there.

STENSGARD. I am not interested in women. It is political matters that I must concentrate on.

HEIRE. She's got bags of money.

STENSGARD. Has she?

HEIRE. Tons of the stuff. And she will be the biggest hen in the coop as soon as the Storli house of cards comes tumbling down.

STENSGARD. What are you on about?

HEIRE. Are you not listening to the gossip? Uninvited guests at Monsen's house. Whispers about police and creditors and false accounting.

STENSGARD. But I was with Monsen only yesterday and he didn't say anything about it to me. Although he did... Do you know the Chamberlain's signature?

STENSGARD *takes the bill out of his pocket and hands it to* HEIRE.

HEIRE. Oh yes, I know it very well.

STENSGARD. Have a look at this.

HEIRE. No, that is not his signature.

STENSGARD. That is what Lundestad said too. Do you really think it is possible that Erik has forged it?

HEIRE. That's not the son's signature either.

STENSGARD. Isn't it?

HEIRE. Absolutely not. What were you planning to do with this?

STENSGARD. Nothing.

HEIRE. Well, it could come in handy.

STENSGARD. Go on.

HEIRE. You could use it to light your cigar.

> STENSGARD *takes the bill back from* HEIRE *and puts it back in his pocket.*

STENSGARD. I don't understand what is happening. First it is Bratsberg who is meant to be sunk, and now Monsen.

HEIRE. Do not worry about it. The moment you think you know how money works and that you can ride it to the land of milk and honey, is the moment that you end up being dashed against the rocks.

STENSGARD. And so the Chamberlain is in the clear?

HEIRE. Oh no! Those who are involved in speculation are like beads on a string. Once one rolls off the rest soon follow.

> LUNDESTAD *enters.*

It is the dependable old peasant stock that ploughs the straightest furrow. So have you persuaded enough to stick with you, Lundestad?

LUNDESTAD. We shall see. It is very tight. Though Stensgard seems to be doing well.

STENSGARD. Even if our pact is successful, I cannot see how I am to find a wife who has any money.

LUNDESTAD. Then Parliament will have to wait.

STENSGARD. No. I cannot effect change without real power.

LUNDESTAD. Well, the vote will have finished by now. Let us see how the count is going.

> ASLAKSEN *enters with a tray of champagne.*

ASLAKSEN. More champagne everyone! Madam Rundholm is footing the bill.

STENSGARD (*in a bolt of inspiration*). You go ahead, Lundestad.

LUNDESTAD *exits into the voting area, followed by* HEIRE.

ASLAKSEN. What a woman she is.

STENSGARD *goes over to the desk and begins to write a letter.*

Are you composing your victory speech, Mr Stensgard? We will need something inspiring for the papers. Oh, how the circulation is going to increase now that we will have something new to talk about.

BASTIAN *enters again and comes over to* ASLAKSEN.

Our movement is in the ascendancy, Bastian.

BASTIAN. Excellent, comrade, and who knows how far our new-found liberty can go. Here is the letter. Make sure you give it to her tonight.

ASLAKSEN. Don't worry. Now have a drink. Come on!

BASTIAN. Of course!

He pours a drink for himself and ASLAKSEN.

We have finally learnt how to stand up for ourselves.

STENSGARD. Aslaksen! Come here. Quickly!

ASLAKSEN *goes over to* STENSGARD *at the table.*

Will you see Madam Rundholm tomorrow?

ASLAKSEN. Oh yes. There's bound to be a few bottles left over.

STENSGARD. Then give her this.

ASLAKSEN. What is it?

STENSGARD. It is some information I promised her. I thought it best to wait until the excitement of today is over.

BASTIAN. Here, Stensgard. You have worked hard enough for the cause. Now it is time to celebrate. Let us all sit together.

STENSGARD *and* ASLAKSEN *join* BASTIAN *at another table*.

STENSGARD. It is too early to be sure of anything.

BASTIAN. Have you spoken to Madam Rundholm?

STENSGARD. A little.

BASTIAN. And how did she respond?

STENSGARD. We were interrupted, I could not tell. But it is always best not to be too confident in oneself.

BASTIAN. What do you mean? Everyone knows she is looking for a husband.

STENSGARD. Well, there are always reasons that no one can foresee; and women... who can truly understand their whims and reasoning? Now please, one last favour. Bastian, my dear comrade, return to the people and judge their mood for me.

BASTIAN. To sense their optimism as we await our moment of glory?

STENSGARD. You are always one step ahead of me.

BASTIAN. Of course! Victory will be ours, Stensgard! And victory for the people; the common people. Those who have nothing and who are nothing. Who are bound up in chains and... by God I feel it!

BASTIAN *knocks back the champagne and exits*.

ASLAKSEN. If he is successful with Madam Rundholm then we will have to put up with even more of his nonsense.

STENSGARD. What do you know of his interest in her?

ASLAKSEN. I have a letter that he wants me to hand over. A plea, I am sure. He has told me of your support for him and he is very grateful.

STENSGARD. So, you have two letters to give her?

ASLAKSEN. I may often be scorned but I know my uses.

STENSGARD. And you have reminded me that I have not written all that I need to in mine. If you could let me have it.

ASLAKSEN *hands him a letter as* MADAM RUNDHOLM *enters.*

ASLAKSEN. And what is it that she wants to know?

STENSGARD. It is politics, Aslaksen. That is all.

MADAM RUNDHOLM. The officials have nearly finalised the count. We will all know the result soon.

STENSGARD *goes up to* MADAM RUNDHOLM.

STENSGARD. For you, madam. Please read it when you are alone. The sooner the better.

MADAM RUNDHOLM. I will, Mr Stensgard. With pleasure.

MADAM RUNDHOLM *exits as* FJELDBO *enters.*

FJELDBO. You have managed to drag out every young pup in the town.

STENSGARD. Each movement needs its footsoldiers.

FJELDBO. And your manoeuvring seems to have paid off. The word is that you will have carried the day.

STENSGARD. Let us wait for the vote to be announced.

FJELDBO. It is a pity you have burnt your bridges with the Chamberlain. You will soon find that you need his support if you really want to get anything done.

STENSGARD. His power is draining away.

FJELDBO. The established order never goes quietly, Stensgard; however wounded you may think they are.

STENSGARD. I have something for the Chamberlain, actually, Fjeldbo.

He reaches into his pocket and takes out the envelope with the bill in it.

FJELDBO. What is it?

STENSGARD. You will be with him tomorrow for his birthday celebrations?

FJELDBO. Of course.

STENSGARD. Then please tell him that now our battle is over I beg his forgiveness and look forward to doing whatever I can to be of service to him.

FJELDBO. What is it you are really striving for?

STENSGARD. You can still join me, Fjeldbo. We need not be enemies. This is a time for men of our generation.

MONSEN *enters*.

MONSEN. Champagne for all!

STENSGARD. Monsen!

MONSEN. Champagne Monsen! Moneybags Monsen!

FJELDBO *exits*.

Oh, what a deal I have pulled off. Spectacular! We will all eat like kings tomorrow at Storli; everyone is invited. Now, where is Madam Rundholm?

STENSGARD. No!

MONSEN. What's wrong, Stensgard?

STENSGARD. Nothing! Nothing at all!

MADAM RUNDHOLM *enters with* LUNDESTAD *and* HEIRE.

MADAM RUNDHOLM. The vote has been announced.

MONSEN. And will our wily old farmer still be making his annual Independence Day speech?

MADAM RUNDHOLM. He is in second place with fifty-three votes.

STENSGARD. Who else was elected with Lundestad?

MADAM RUNDHOLM. In first place, joining Mr Lundestad at the assembly, and therefore eligible to be selected to sit in Parliament, with a total of one hundred and seventeen votes...

STENSGARD. It's the dean, isn't it? No, not the dean but the district councillor!

MADAM RUNDHOLM....is Mr Stensgard!

STENSGARD *jumps up on the table.*

STENSGARD. Then a toast, my friends! A toast to the train of liberty that is soon to leave the station.

ASLAKSEN. Speech! Speech!

HEIRE. Oh no, we've had too many of those lately. Surely now we can get on with our lives again.

ASLAKSEN. He's right. Champagne! Champagne!

LUNDESTAD. And will there be a wife on board this train, Mr Stensgard?

STENSGARD. Oh, most definitely. In fact, there could even be three.

We hear the popping of champagne corks as the lights go out.

We now see SERVANTS *in the shadows moving the furniture around. It is the following day and they are laying out a party in a reception room at* BRATSBERG's. *There is a door at the back and a door to the side.*

The lights come up on the corner of the stage to show ERIK *sitting on a chair alone with his head in his hands.* SELMA *enters.*

SELMA. Another big day for your father. He seems to be having a lot of them lately.

ERIK. Yes...

SELMA. What is it?

ERIK. Nothing. Go and see if Thora is ready.

SELMA. No. Tell me. Erik. What's the matter?

ERIK. I'm ruined. That's all.

SELMA. What is ruined?

ERIK. Everything. All of it has gone.

SELMA. Do you mean your money?

ERIK. Yes. I have borrowed too and cannot pay that back. And I have done something...

SELMA. What?

ERIK. It doesn't matter. None of it matters. Only that I am destroyed, Selma. I am destroyed totally; money, inheritance and honour.

SELMA. And your father knows of this?

ERIK. Of course he does! (*Has a sudden realisation and jumps to his feet*.) Come, let us leave together. You are the only one I have left now. We must face misfortune hand in hand.

SELMA *begins to laugh*.

Why are you laughing? For God's sake, why are you laughing?

SELMA. So now I am finally good enough?

ERIK. What is this, Selma?

SELMA. I despise you.

ERIK. You don't mean that.

SELMA. Yes I do, Erik.

ERIK. I am sorry... listen... please, I was only trying to prove myself... to try and...

SELMA. I have always been the pauper of this family. Always the one that was expected to take and never allowed to give. Not once have I been asked to make any kind of sacrifice because I was never good enough to face anything. That is why I hate you, Erik.

ERIK. You are ill.

SELMA. How I have longed to share your troubles. But whenever I asked if anything was wrong you sent me away with a silly little joke. You dressed me like a doll; you played with me like you play with a child. And I wanted to help carry the burden. To be able to experience the turmoil and triumphs of life. And now finally you ask me. Finally I am good enough, when you have nothing. Well, it is too late! I don't want to be the one you reach out for at the very end. I don't want your troubles, Erik. I would rather dance and sing in the streets.

SELMA *exits*. FJELDBO *enters*.

FJELDBO. Good morning.

ERIK. Oh, you.

FJELDBO. Are all the preparations ready for the Chamberlain's birthday?

ERIK. What does it matter?

FJELDBO. May I ask how things are between you and your father?

ERIK. What do you think?

FJELDBO. And you have heard about Monsen?

ERIK. Of course. Buying champagne for everyone. Celebrating his great success. With the money of others.

FJELDBO. And when they all went to bed he ran away.

ERIK. What do you mean?

FJELDBO. He wanted to fool everybody so that he could escape. It was timber that brought him down in the end. Huge losses.

ERIK. That's where all of my money has gone too, then.

FJELDBO. But now that he has left you will not have to pay the interest on any loan he may have made to you.

ERIK. Where is he?

FJELDBO. In Sweden probably. The authorities turned up at Storli this morning. The contents were listed and the house sealed.

ERIK. And the family?

FJELDBO. Thora has brought Ragna here and is to ask your father if he will help her. There is no word of the son.

BRATSBERG *enters*.

Good morning, Chamberlain. And may I wish you many happy returns on your birthday.

BRATSBERG. I don't think there's much cause for happiness, do you? And from now on I am not to be referred to as Chamberlain; I am simply the owner of the ironworks.

FJELDBO. Why?

BRATSBERG. I like to think there is still some honour in this town, doctor. I plan to let the King know that the esteem in which he has always held my family has been a blessing that is no longer deserved. Our name is disgraced just as much as Mr Monsen's.

FJELDBO. And I fear that with Stensgard's election we shall lose even more of our good character.

BRATSBERG. Maybe you are right. I do not think we understand what moral judgement is any more.

FJELDBO. Oh, he asked me to give you something.

He hands over the envelope with the bill in. BRATSBERG *takes it.*

I have known him since we were boys, at the grammar school. He received a scholarship which filled him with high aspirations, even though at home he lived a coarse and bitter life, with a layabout father and a mother who worked herself into exhaustion. It was bound to lead to a split personality. And now we see the results. A man who behaves one way in his thoughts and feelings and another entirely in his actions. And I do not think he is even aware of it.

BRATSBERG. And that is your diagnosis then, doctor?

FJELDBO. Well, yes. And I understand this because I have had the good fortune to experience an upbringing necessary to instil stability of character. A peaceful and harmonious family who never overstretched themselves, no excesses of thought or emotion to get in the way...

BRATSBERG. Which is why you are so perfect?

FJELDBO. I am not saying that, Chamberlain... Mr Bratsberg... but circumstances have favoured me more than he and I hope that you can see that I am a man who is of worth.

BRATSBERG. Unlike that scoundrel Stensgard?

FJELDBO. Yes.

BRATSBERG. That scoundrel who has the nobility of character to send me my son's forged bill.

FJELDBO. Has he?

ERIK. Where?

BRATSBERG. Here.

ERIK. It was a mistake, Father. I was pressured into it... I did not understand... truly understand... what I was doing. Believe me; please believe...

BRATSBERG. Just take it! And do what you will with the wretched thing.

ERIK. Thank you, Father. I am saved.

BRATSBERG. Oh, Erik, is this all that it now takes for a man's conscience to be cleared?

ERIK. I must tell Selma. She will understand, I know it. Poor, sweet Selma. It has all been a terrible mistake.

ERIK *exits*.

BRATSBERG. Did he pass on any message with this?

FJELDBO. Yes. That now the battle is over he begs your forgiveness and looks forward to doing whatever he can to be of service to you.

BRATSBERG. Well, then maybe things are turning out better than I thought. From this day forward, doctor, my house will be open to him. Maybe he and Thora would make a good match after all.

FJELDBO. Please, Chamberlain... Mr Bratsberg... I beg of you to think again.

BRATSBERG. What is it with you, Fjeldbo? I cannot put my finger on it but there is something about you that always annoys me. At least Stensgard is direct and doesn't sneak around trying to ingratiate himself with everyone.

LUNDESTAD *enters*.

LUNDESTAD. Good morning, Chamberlain. And may I wish you every honour on this...

BRATSBERG. Oh, be quiet, Lundestad. Although congratulations are in order. I hear you limped through the election and will soon be handing over your seat in Parliament to Stensgard.

LUNDESTAD. It all went according to my intentions.

FJELDBO. Did it?

BRATSBERG *fires a look at* FJELDBO *indicating that he has no right to be involved in this conversation.* FJELDBO *meekly withdraws and stands silent as the conversation continues around him.*

LUNDESTAD. Oh yes, you do not cross someone like Stensgard. He has something that the rest of us would give our right arm for.

BRATSBERG. And what is that?

LUNDESTAD. The ability to sway the crowd. To make them believe that he has their interests at heart. And what makes him even more powerful is that he is not weighed down with social responsibilities. Or indeed convictions. Which makes it very easy for him to be a liberal.

BRATSBERG. And are you saying that you want to support all this revolutionary business?

LUNDESTAD. Once new ideas have sprung up, it's very difficult to bury them again. Which is why you have to get along with them as best as you can.

BRATSBERG. But we represent the solid traditional Norwegian decency.

LUNDESTAD. And I will, of course, be as obstructive as I can. But he does have real influence. And your son's bill, of course; which he could use at any time to his advantage.

BRATSBERG. Oh no, he has sent that to me.

LUNDESTAD. Has he?

BRATSBERG. As an olive branch.

LUNDESTAD. I am surprised.

BRATSBERG. We have all underestimated him. Maybe power has civilised him, Lundestad, as it civilised you.

STENSGARD *appears in the doorway at the back of the stage.*

STENSGARD. May I be allowed to approach?

BRATSBERG. You may safely do so.

STENSGARD. And will you accept my congratulations?

BRATSBERG. I will indeed. And I should congratulate you.

They shake hands.

STENSGARD. Thank you... thank you. Did the doctor here pass on my message?

BRATSBERG. He did. And from this day forward, if you wish it, my home is your home.

There is a knock at the door.

Enter!

Several local MEN *and* WOMEN *arrive to greet*
BRATSBERG, *including* HEIRE, THORA *and* RAGNA.
THORA *goes up to* STENSGARD.

THORA. Mr Stensgard, Erik has just told me of your actions.
We have misjudged you, all of us. I would dearly like to
know how I could make amends.

STENSGARD. There is a one thing you could do for me, Miss
Bratsberg.

THORA. And what is that?

STENSGARD. Not now. I will ask you later. When you have
come to know me more.

BRATSBERG. Refreshments are served!

The MAIDS *appear with wine and cakes as* THORA *goes
back into the* CROWD *to talk to* RAGNA. STENSGARD
goes over to LUNDESTAD.

STENSGARD. Ah, Lundestad, I feel like a victorious god! First
my triumph at the elections and now… well, let us just say
that all that I have been striving for is to come to pass.

LUNDESTAD. Then Miss Monsen has agreed to your
marriage?

STENSGARD. Ragna?

LUNDESTAD. Bastian told me that he was putting in a word
for you. He was sure that she would say yes.

STENSGARD. But in the middle of a family scandal her mind
will be… confused. I would not want to take advantage of
such a thing. And perhaps there is another match to be made.
One that, given the ever-changing circumstances, will ensure
that our pact remains firm.

HEIRE *has come over to* STENSGARD.

HEIRE. Congratulations, Mr Stensgard.

STENSGARD. That was yesterday's news.

LUNDESTAD *moves away.*

HEIRE. Oh, I'm not talking of that nonsense. You've reeled her in, my friend, good and proper. Well done.

STENSGARD. Who?

HEIRE. Madam Rundholm! I saw her this morning, fresh as a daisy, waving a letter and laughing like a madwoman. She told me everything.

STENSGARD. What did she say?

HEIRE. That the letter was an offer of marriage. And that she was now engaged to a most talented man.

STENSGARD. Oh no.

HEIRE. Is there something the matter?

STENSGARD. Please, I beg of you, don't mention a word of this to anyone.

HEIRE. Why not?

STENSGARD. Because… I am a man much in demand, Mr Heire. There is a lady here that I will need to let down very lightly. If you see what I mean.

HEIRE. Of course. A statesman and a dandy. Some men have all the luck.

HEIRE *goes across to* LUNDESTAD *and begins to talk to him.* STENSGARD *knocks back a drink. He seems uncomfortable, slightly cornered now.* LUNDESTAD *and* HEIRE *go over to* BRATSBERG *as* FJELDBO *comes over to* STENSGARD.

FJELDBO. So, you were even able to use me.

STENSGARD. Look at them – Bratsberg, Lundestad and Heire. All of them once high and mighty men. And do you know what they will be talking about? Me. Because this may appear to be a celebration to mark the Chamberlain's birthday, but it is not. It is the moment when I am introduced to all as the new force in this community. Now excuse me whilst I go and talk to Miss Bratsberg, who I hope very soon to be married to.

STENSGARD *moves away and joins* THORA *and* RAGNA.

BRATSBERG. Doctor – over here! Listen to this and tell me what you think.

FJELDBO. Oh, I would not want to ingratiate myself, Chamberlain... Mr Bratsberg.

BRATSBERG. Stop feeling sorry for yourself and do as you're told.

FJELDBO *goes over to join them.*

Did you talk to Stensgard before he gave you the bill?

FJELDBO. What does it matter? Why is everyone so interested in this man? Can't any of you see?

LUNDESTAD. Daniel here says that he told Stensgard that the bill was no good. That he should light his cigar with it.

HEIRE. And why not? I could see that the Chamberlain's signature was forged so there's no reason why Erik's couldn't have been too.

BRATSBERG. But it wasn't. And you know that.

HEIRE. And you know I like stirring things up, just to have a little bit of fun. There's not a lot else to do when you're this old and you have no money.

LUNDESTAD. It must be that Stensgard thought he could no longer use the bill to threaten the Chamberlain.

BRATSBERG. I'll ask you again, doctor. Did you talk to Stensgard before he gave you the bill?

FJELDBO. I simply said that it was a shame that he had burnt his bridges with you. That he would need your support to get anything done.

BRATSBERG. So once again it is you that has precipitated everything.

FJELDBO. No! That is not fair!

BRATSBERG. And once again I have been used by that man and taken for a fool.

HEIRE. I don't think that any of us can argue with that.

BRATSBERG (*to* LUNDESTAD). And this is the person that you have protected and promoted and advanced. This is the person who you have collaborated with.

LUNDESTAD. And so have you.

BRATSBERG. What's he doing?

FJELDBO. Talking with your daughter.

BRATSBERG. And he dare think that… Right… Doctor, I am giving you the honour of getting rid of our newly elected guest.

FJELDBO. Me?

BRATSBERG. Yes.

FJELDBO. Get rid of Stensgard?

BRATSBERG. Absolutely.

FJELDBO. In whatever way I like?

BRATSBERG. Yes, man! I give you absolute freedom to attack him in any way you wish.

FJELDBO. Thank you, Chamberlain. I need a drink.

They shake hands and FJELDBO *moves away to get a drink.*

LUNDESTAD. What do you think he will do?

BRATSBERG. I have no idea. They are two idiots together. Let them create the stir and then we will have done with it.

LUNDESTAD. We have both made fools of ourselves.

BRATSBERG. Yes, yes, we have. But enough is enough, Lundestad. This entire League of Youth nonsense must come to an end. Ladies and gentlemen, your attention please! I know that we are here to celebrate my birthday, but we also have in our midst our conquering hero, Mr Stensgard. I think it is fair to say that all of us here have at times been unsure of who exactly he is, and indeed what exactly he stands for. But I think it is also fair to say that we have all finally come to understand his true character.

Cries of 'Hear, hear!' from amongst the GUESTS.

STENSGARD. I thank you most sincerely, Chamberlain. And I understand how fractious this election may have been, how it has stirred up feelings within the district, feelings that may have lain dormant for many years. But now that it is over and I have won, I promise that I will listen to all of you. That my door will be open.

BRATSBERG. But one moment please, Mr Stensgard. Your oratory is as usual most interesting but we must first let Doctor Fjeldbo speak.

STENSGARD. Fjeldbo?

BRATSBERG. Oh yes. Doctor Fjeldbo has something he would like to say.

FJELDBO. Now?

BRATSBERG. This is the chance you have been waiting for. And we are all listening very carefully, doctor. So please don't make a mess of it. And speak up, man!

FJELDBO. My friends, I have the honour, with the consent of the Chamberlain, of announcing my engagement to his daughter.

There is surprise and excitement amongst the GUESTS. THORA *has a huge smile on her face as she comes forward to* BRATSBERG *whilst he is holding in his anger at being outflanked by* FJELDBO.

STENSGARD. Your engagement?

LUNDESTAD. To the doctor?

THORA. Thank you, Father.

BRATSBERG. Well, it appears that we are all living in a time of new associations. Perhaps I should also join the League of Youth.

LUNDESTAD. Mr Stensgard, without a marriage that will bring you what you need, I will be unable to hand over power to you. I suggest that you forget all about Parliament for now.

BRATSBERG. And I think it's time that you left.

STENSGARD. Look at you all! With your smug self-satisfied faces. How can anyone hope to break into this circle, this cabal of wealth and privilege without having to play games, without having to get one's hands dirty? Something that you never do, Chamberlain, because you simply ask others to do it for you. A nod here, a handshake there and any new idea that comes along is simply smothered to death in its cot. Well, not this time. I will not be crushed underfoot by you. I am the victor, Chamberlain. I have been given a mandate to work for the good of the people and I intend to tie myself through the strings of my heart to those people. And that is why I also have an engagement to announce.

FJELDBO. Engaged?

HEIRE. I bear witness!

LUNDESTAD. But just now you said that you would have nothing to do with Miss Monsen.

RAGNA. Me?

BRATSBERG. Well, there would be some honour in that, Mr Stensgard, seeing that her family is now utterly humiliated.

THORA. Father!

FJELDBO. Finally you show us a decent side to your character.

BRATSBERG. Why are you being so charitable to the man?

FJELDBO. Now that I am to be as a son to you, I hope to exhibit the Bratsberg beneficence.

LUNDESTAD. Well done, Stensgard!

BRATSBERG. Yes. Why not put this sordid business behind us once and for all. Go ahead and marry Miss Monsen. Somebody has to deal with her; and it will keep you out of Parliament.

LUNDESTAD. Three cheers for Stensgard. Hip hip!

The cheering starts.

STENSGARD. No! No! You misunderstand. It is not Miss Monsen that I am engaged to, it is Madam Rundholm.

BRATSBERG. The shopkeeper's widow?

STENSGARD. That is all she may be to you, but that is because you are unable to see her true worth.

HEIRE. I'd like to see that!

FJELDBO. But what about poor Ragna?

RAGNA. Leave me alone!

RAGNA *runs out of the room, crying.*

STENSGARD. Madam Rundholm is a woman of riper years, a woman whose experience of life will put meat on the bones of my ideals; who will give me a home, who will support me in my position as a humble man of the people.

HEIRE. And she's the richest woman in the district.

LUNDESTAD. Then it appears that you have been successful after all, Mr Stensgard.

STENSGARD. And we will stick to our deal?

LUNDESTAD. Yes.

BRATSBERG. He has won?

LUNDESTAD. He has.

ASLAKSEN *enters.*

ASLAKSEN. I do beg your pardon.

BRATSBERG. Oh, Aslaksen. Come on through.

ASLAKSEN. I am sorry, sir, but I was hoping to speak to Mr Stensgard. It's important that we let the people know what is happening.

BRATSBERG. You are right. Your paper must print a portrait of the new leader and champion of our community. God help us.

MADAM RUNDHOLM *appears at the door.*

THORA. Look. Here she is.

MADAM RUNDHOLM. I just came to congratulate you, Chamberlain. I did not realise you had so many guests.

BRATSBERG. Come in. It's we that should congratulate you.

MADAM RUNDHOLM. You have heard, then?

LUNDESTAD. I only hope that you know what you are letting yourself in for.

MADAM RUNDHOLM. He may have had reason to be ridiculed in the past but he has a great future ahead.

BRATSBERG. And one that puts us all in danger. I am surprised that a woman of your experience could be so taken in.

STENSGARD. Ignore them. To be betrothed is a beautiful thing.

MADAM RUNDHOLM. Are you engaged too? And I know that his first bridge was a disaster but I'm sure that his next one will hold.

FJELDBO. Isn't Stensgard the man that you are to marry, Madam Rundholm?

MADAM RUNDHOLM. Why would I want to do that?

STENSGARD. I demand to know what is happening.

MADAM RUNDHOLM. For a moment I did think I was being propositioned. But then he gave me a letter from Bastian.

STENSGARD. Aslaksen. Have you anything in your pocket?

ASLAKSEN *takes out a letter from his pocket which* STENSGARD *grabs.*

ASLAKSEN. Ah yes, of course, I was going to hand it over but what with one thing and another, and all the excite...

STENSGARD *crushes the letter in his fingers.*

STENSGARD. Damn you! You gave me back the wrong one.

BRATSBERG. So what will our 'man of the people' do now? Perhaps you can go and drink a beer with them.

LUNDESTAD. Or eat a sausage.

FJELDBO. Or go and smoke some of their tobacco.

STENSGARD. You must please all excuse me. Urgent business awaits.

FJELDBO. And may I suggest it is the last business that you do in this town.

STENSGARD. But I have been elected.

LUNDESTAD. And will never be chosen for Parliament now. If you stay here you will simply while away your hours making decisions about paperweights.

BRATSBERG. And we wouldn't want to waste a man of such immense talents on such a thing would we?

The assembled GUESTS *all shout 'No!'*

LUNDESTAD. I'm sure we can find someone to take your place. Perhaps the dean or the district councillor.

STENSGARD. Then I take my leave of you and your town. May it slowly sink into a puddle of mediocrity.

STENSGARD *leaves.*

BRATSBERG. Well, everyone, I think that I'll tear up my resignation to the King and continue as I was for the good of the community.

LUNDESTAD. And if you are prepared to work for the benefit of the district, then it would certainly be a great shame if I should desert my duty.

BRATSBERG. Then a toast, my friends. To good old
Lundestad!

HEIRE. The old ones are always the best.

As they carry out their toast, SELMA *has come into the
room with* ERIK.

BRATSBERG. And here is my son. With whom I have decided
to go into business.

ERIK. Yes, Father.

BRATSBERG. Selma, your husband will make a success of
himself yet.

SELMA. Let us hope so.

BRATSBERG. This is a celebration. Why do you look so
uncertain?

SELMA. Maybe I am not as sure as the rest of you that
everything is quite as it was before.

LUNDESTAD. She is right. Men like Stensgard will always
worm their way into power. We may have seen the back of
him here, but there will always be another town just like ours
waiting to welcome him in.

BRATSBERG. But by the time he does get real power he'll be
too old to lead the League of Youth. You never know – he
may even end up like us!

*The gathering all raise their glasses and shout 'Skol!' as the
lights fade out.*

Fin.

A Nick Hern Book

This version of *The League of Youth* first published in Great Britain as a paperback original in 2011 by Nick Hern Books Limited, 14 Larden Road, London W3 7ST, in association with Nottingham Playhouse

This version of *The League of Youth* copyright © 2011 Andy Barrett

Andy Barrett has asserted his right to be identified as the author of this version

Cover image by Tom Partridge with Sam Callis as Stensgard (front), Robin Kingsland as Monsen and Philip Bretherton as Bratsberg (back)
Cover design by Ned Hoste, 2H

Typeset by Nick Hern Books, London
Printed and bound by CLE Print Ltd, St Ives, Cambs, PE27 3LE

A CIP catalogue record for this book is available from the British Library

ISBN   978 1 84842 188 2

FSC
www.fsc.org
MIX
From responsible sources
FSC® C019549